HOT LIPS

HOT LIPS

THE
ULTIMATE
KISS AND TELL
~ BOOK ~

Noëlle Walsh

EBURY PRESS

Published by Ebury Press
National Magazine House
72 Broadwick Street
London W1V 2BP

First impression 1985

ISBN 0 85223 447 3

Computerset in Great Britain by
MFK Typesetting Ltd., Saffron Walden, Essex

Printed and bound in Great Britain by
Butler & Tanner Ltd., Frome

CONTENTS

SCREEN KISSES

In today's cinema, a kiss is like an overture to the full orchestral symphony which follows, leaving the audience panting with anticipation for the real business to come. Modern cinematic kisses rain down indiscriminately on throat, breasts, stomach, toes – a far cry from the Hollywood heyday of the Thirties and Forties when the face and shoulders were their only sanctuary. Then, a kiss was like an abbreviation, implying more than it could ever portray.

The censorship-sensitive mood of the pre- and post-war decades decreed that a passionate embrace should signal a discreet fade-out. As the curtain closed, the kiss offered brief but tantalising foreplay for the cinema audience's imaginations. To the alert film-goer, though, those carefully choreographed clinches, going far beyond the sexual element, were shorthand for a wide range of emotions from jealousy and duplicity to evil and love.

The modern revival in celluloid kisses harks back to the body-crushing clinches of Valentino and the manipulative mouth-meeting of the great screen vamps. Love and passion were the stock-in-trades of the early cinema, bringing with them a host of new screen heroes and

Swooning, limp, but expectant feminity prepares herself to receive the ravaging attentions of the Desert Prince in The Sheik, *Valentino's most famous film.*

heroines whose main claim to fame was their osculatory talent.

Passionate and predatory, the most famous screen vamps of the Twenties were foreign in origin – as if their un-Americanness allowed them to display their most basic passions. With just a twitch of their lips, actresses like Theda Bara, Pola Negri and Nita Naldi made strong men into drooling babies.

Theda Bara, the prototype for all future screen vamps, reduced three men to pulp in *A Fool There Was* (1915). Like those Barbara Cartland heroines, who faint away at the merest touch of the hero's lips, Theda's kisses literally sucked a man dry. In one scene, she enters a room

♡

CHAMPAGNE AND SLIPPERS

When the incredibly rich Aly Khan married Rita Hayworth in France in 1949, 15 bottles of Champagne were earmarked for each guest and Rita was given a cash dowry, a quartet of race horses, an Alfa-Romeo, and assorted diamonds and rubies. Aly capped the occasion by leaning forward during the reception and kissing Rita's slipper.

as the wife of the married man with whom she is having an affair pleads with her husband to forget his mistress. Stepping between them, Theda grabs the husband and kisses him long and passionately – it was one of the longest screen kisses at the time, lasting almost two minutes – while the wife stands helplessly by. Afterwards, Theda turns to the wife and laughingly dares her to try and take the husband back – if she can. Meanwhile, the husband sinks to the ground, floored by the passion and power of Theda's kisses.

In the Twenties, screen vamps had enormous power over their leading men. Even cinematic heroes like Valentino occasionally fell victim to these female predators. But Valentino escaped the clutches of evil feminity by taking the role of screen vamp for himself. In *The Sheik* (1921), his most famous film, he enslaved thousands of female hearts with his all-consuming possession of the young heroine.

The Sheik was not only a turning-

Famous leading man, as well as ladies' man, John Barrymore shocked fans with his manic portrayal of the darker side of the gentle medical man in Doctor Jekyll and Mr Hyde.

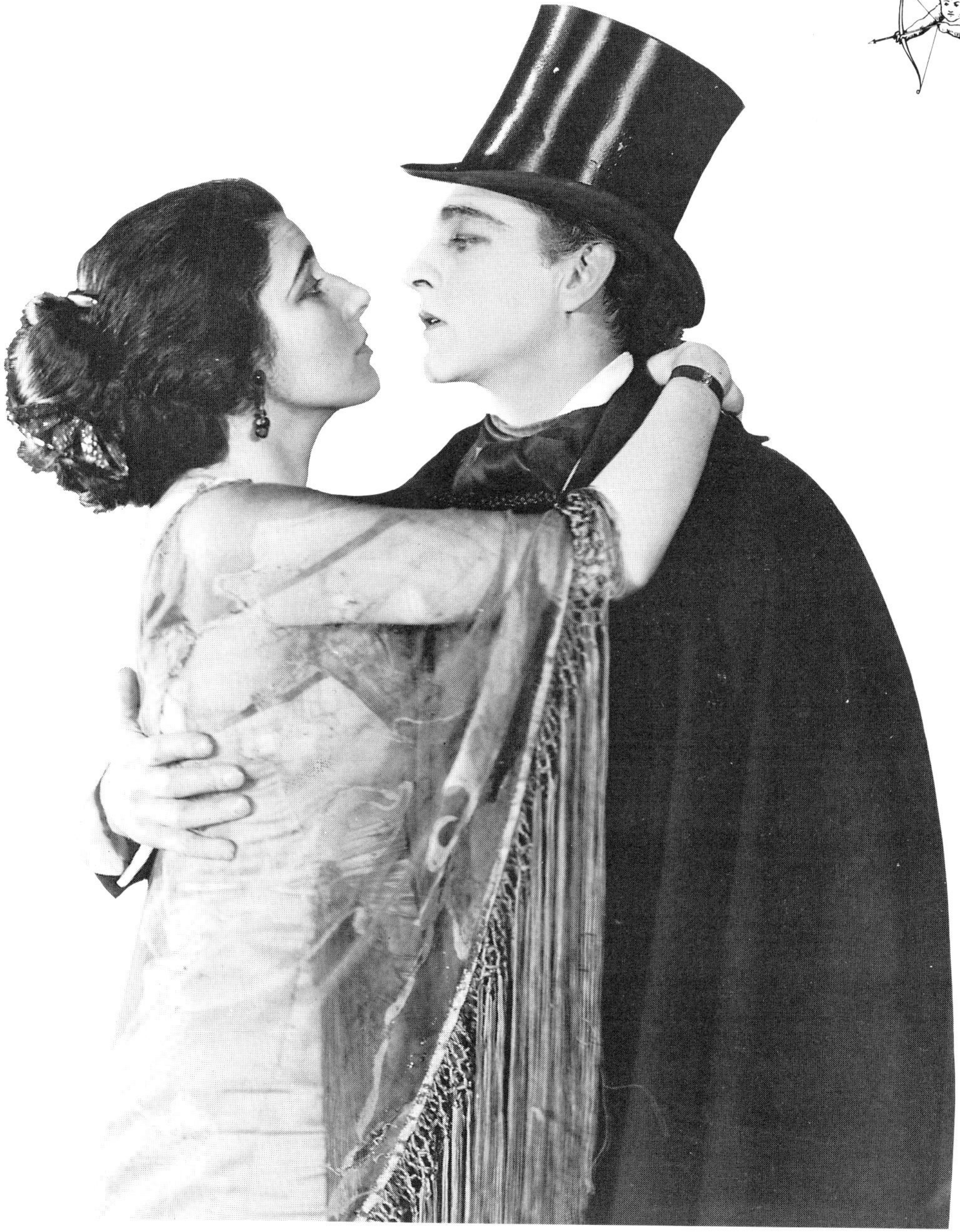

point for Valentino – assuring his image as the great screen lover – it also provided the most daring cinematic embrace of the Silent Screen, when the olive-skinned Sheik kidnaps a white girl, takes her to his tent and seduces her. The male vamp's style of kissing was of the widened eyeball, hypnotic gaze and distended nostril variety. But the touch of his lips was enough to rob any woman of the power to resist. The script for the seduction scene in *The Sheik* shows Valentino's ability to overcome female moral scruples. 'She withered in his arms as he crushed her to him in a sudden access of passion. His head bent slowly down to her, his eyes burned deeper and, held immovable, she endured the first kiss she had ever received. And the touch of his scorching lips, the clasp of his arms, the close union with his warm, strong body robbed her of all strength and of all power of resistance.' (Later, the film censors were to outlaw seduction scenes between sexes of different colour.)

Valentino's appeal responded to the more relaxed libido of the war-liberated era he dominated, and his Mediterranean good looks were a good counter-balance to the virginal

NO NECKING

In 1937, the Production Code Administration looked at 6,663 full-length domestic feature scripts and films, saving the public from such licentious scenes as kisses on the neck and shoulder, and women and men lying together on a bed.

fragility of the early screen heroines who fought bitterly to fend off his advances, but succumbed in the end to his romantic menace. Unlike modern films, which are primarily designed for the arousal of men, Valentino's films were geared towards the arousal of women. With women constituting the cinema's most sizeable and loyal audience, studio bosses couldn't afford to ignore them. Special scenes were devised to enable Valentino to show off his physique – kept in trim by daily two-hour workouts.

All the best screen vamps had staying power and Valentino was no exception. At one time, film censors decreed that a kiss should not last longer than 'one yard of film'. Translated, that was 36 seconds. Valentino had a reputation for using up every last inch of this three-foot allowance. Unfortunately, his off-screen love life wasn't as successful as his on-screen romances – his first wife locked him out on their wedding night, refusing to consummate the marriage. He died in 1926, at the early age of 31, from peritonitis.

EVIL KISSES

One way in which particularly voracious kisses were able to by-pass the censors was to de-sex the seducer by making him a monster: a vampire, for example. Directors first conceived the idea after watching the 1920 version of *Dr Jekyll and Mr Hyde* with the legendary John Barrymore. As the gentle Dr Jekyll, Barrymore's intimate encounters with the heroine were models of chivalry. But as the evil Mr Hyde, complete with claw-like hands and fang-like teeth, he became a sadistic sex maniac, grabbing her viciously in kisses of heady passion.

Barrymore shocked audiences at the time with the intensity of his kisses. (Later, Barrymore was to shock co-stars in a different way. Joan Crawford said that although she loved playing opposite him, she hated their love scenes as his breath always smelled of drink and he often refused to shave, leaving her with a red rash. Barrymore died an alcoholic.)

European films led the way in setting the pattern for the daring vampirish 'sexless' kisses, in particular the German film *Nosferatu* (1921). Based on the Dracula story, the film features a saintly heroine, determined to save her town from being laid to waste by the blood-thirsty Dracula. One night, while reading a book on vampires, she learns that the only way to kill this creature is to keep him in bed until dawn, when the sun will strike him dead. She entices Dracula to her bedroom one

KISSING CUTS

The first Far Eastern country to permit kissing in films was China in 1926 in *Two Women in the House*. In Japan, where kissing was considered 'unclean, immodest, indecorous, ungraceful and likely to spread disease' – at least by Tokyo's Prefect of Police – some 800,000 ft. of kissing scenes were cut from American movies that same year.

night while her husband is away, and lies in bed while the monstrous figure with talon-like teeth and huge, Spock-like ears approaches, kneels down by the bedside, and sinks his fangs into her neck in a bloodcurdling bite-kiss.

This scene was copied in many later vampire films, and proved to be very successful in evading the strict censorship of the following decade. All through the Thirties and Forties, vampires were able simultaneously to bite and kiss ladies by claiming that the kiss was not sexual but merely a hunt for fresh necks to suck.

IMP GIRLS AND IT GIRLS

The Twenties saw the introduction of a host of new screen heroes and heroines who divided up neatly into two groups according to their kissability. One group consisted of the Imp Girls, named after the Imp Film Production Company – coquettish, flirtatious, but ever pure and unkissable, wide-eyed and innocent. Like the original Imp Girl, Florence Lawrence, they might, in generous moods, allow a particularly ardent lover's lips to brush their cheek, but attempts to sneak a kiss on the lips were met with a swift rebuke. When Florence Lawrence's star waned, the golden-ringleted Mary Pickford took over the role of child-woman with the trade papers of the time proclaiming, 'Mary is an Imp now.'

In the other group were the It Girls, epitomised by pert and vivacious Clara Bow in the 1927 film *It*. They were anything but innocent. Like the great screen vamps of the early Twenties, they prided themselves on their lip power. Bow was a tease who drove all her leading men mad with her provocative manner.

In *My Lady of Whims* (1925), a tortured Clive Brook spends the entire film chasing the whimsical Clara. As the film draws to a close, she deliberately falls from her horse, causing our gallant hero to dash to her rescue. 'Are you hurt?' he asks, on reaching her prone figure. 'On my forehead,' she replies prettily, whereupon he places a gentle kiss on the spot. When she points to her hurt nose, he kisses that, too. But the place that hurts most of all is her lips, she sighs in the closing seconds of the film. Clive Brook bends down to kiss them better.

ORAL DEVICES

In the Silent Film era, when the story had to be conveyed visually, screen gestures were vital in helping the audience to follow the plot. Directors used the kiss not only to signify love and passion, but also to show sorrow, loss, revenge and hatred. One information-packed kiss could obviate the need for two or three captions. For example, in D W Griffith's remake of the Faust story, *The Sorrows of Satan* (1926), the audience knows the fate of the hapless hero from the vamp's pre-osculatory gestures.

The action takes place in a nightclub, with the hero seated opposite the wicked but irresistible Lya de

Men were always putty in this famous vamp's hands. Surrounded by the debris of her victim's life, in Sorrows of Satan, *Lya de Putti worked alongside Satan to destroy the hero.*

Putti, who has been commissioned by the Satan character to seduce and corrupt the hero. Lya takes out a cigarette, puts it slowly into her mouth and proceeds to roll it lasciviously around her lips, eye-balling the hero all the time. She then drops the unlit cigarette on the floor and grinds it under her foot, which then slides back under the table and works its way up his leg. When she suggests going somewhere quieter, the audience knows our hero is going to fall prey to her wicked wiles. They go behind some curtains, whereupon she grabs him, her mouth open, and they go into a deep French kiss.

Despite the blatant French kiss – an unusual feature on American screens, although European actors and actresses practised it all the time – this film aroused little controversy. Audiences recognised and assented to the ploys used by silent film-makers – cigarettes, straws, necklaces – in order to shorten the need for dialogue.

John Gilbert's world was turned upside down when Garbo announced the end of their off-screen romance in 1929. At the time of filming Flesh and The Devil, *in 1935, he still hadn't regained his equilibrium, and subsequently fell into an alcoholic decline from which he never recovered.*

15

The Twenties saw a great deal of oral interplay, which usually presaged a kiss. In *Flesh and the Devil* (1927), Garbo used a match to illuminate her desire for John Gilbert. Both are standing in the semi-darkness with cigarettes in their mouths when Gilbert strikes a match. Garbo asks him, via a caption, if he knows what extinguishing a match means. He replies in the negative so she informs him that it is an invitation to kiss a woman. Very deliberately, Gilbert blows out the match and the two go into a very hard kiss.

Garbo and Gilbert were the greatest screen lovers of the Twenties, both on and off-screen. On Valentino's death in 1926, Gilbert took over as the nation's number one heart-throb, his devil-may-care attitude proving to be the stuff of which heroes were made.

Although Garbo liked to star with Gilbert (she turned down Laurence Olivier as her co-star in *Queen Christina*, (1933), in favour of Gilbert), the beginning of the talkies marked the end of their partnership. Gilbert was one of the many casualties of the talkies, although rumour has it that the sound test which revealed his supposedly thin, reedy voice and blocked his entrance to the great Hollywood era, had been 'fixed' by studio boss Louis B Mayer, jealous of Gilbert's growing influence with his top box-office draw.

CENSORED KISSES

As directors became more and more adventurous in depicting sex and passion on the screen, so there was an increasing lobby from conservative bodies, notably the Catholic League of Decency. The League was dissatisfied with the fact that 90 minutes of celluloid sin could be followed by 5 minutes of redemption and still satisfy the censors. It deplored the movie industry's fascination with sex, its preoccupation with the working girl and the emancipation of women, with the discarding of old codes of manners and morals, and with the slackening of marital ties – despite the fact that the erring wives always went back to their patient husbands and the Dancing Daughters eventually married the boys next door.

The Motion Picture Association (MPA) had already drawn up voluntary guidelines as to what should and should not be seen on the screen. But faced with the growing wrath of the

HATED LOVE SCENES

On the screen, steamy love scenes look so convincing, it's easy to believe that the stars really are having a good time. But in many cases, before that perfect kiss was immortalised on celluloid, a lot of teeth clenching went on behind the scenes.

In the 1935 version of *Anna Karenina*, Greta Garbo's treatment of her co-star, Fredric March, showed that, even then, she preferred being alone. Determined that their love scenes would be brief and to the point, Garbo would munch garlic before each clinch.

In an earlier version of the same film (which was renamed *Love* and given a happy ending), Garbo had no such trouble with her co-star, John Gilbert. But as passionate off-screen lovers, their screen embraces didn't require an overdose of acting ability. Unfortunately, Gilbert's love affair with Garbo was to be his downfall. Worried at Gilbert's growing influence with his top star, studio boss Louis B. Mayer is reputed to have made sure that when talkies were introduced, Gilbert failed his sound test. Gilbert's career – and his love affair with Garbo – foundered and he died in the mid-1930s from alcoholism.

Forty years later, taking a leaf out of Garbo's book, Diana Rigg (right) also used the garlic clove to cut short her hated love

scenes with one-time-only 007, George Lazenby.

17

powerful League and the threat of a cinema boycott by millions of Catholics, the MPA set up the Production Code Administration under Will Hays. This organisation read all film scripts, advised as to the undesirable elements in the scripts and proclaimed upon the acceptability of finished films. Acceptable films were given the 'seal' without which their distribution prospects would be severely restricted.

Among many actions 'outlawed' by the Production Code, or Hays Code as it became known, was 'excessive and lustful kissing' – widely taken to mean French kissing. In fact, few American film stars practised open-mouth kissing on the screen. It was left to Franco-German films like *Casanova* (1942) to show close-ups of French kisses. Actresses like Louise Brooks, who began her career in foreign films, had to revert to closed mouth kissing when she returned to the American cinema.

The rules were gradually relaxed after the Second World War, and in 1956, a review of the Production Code positively prohibited only 3 subjects: venereal disease, sexual perversion and foul language. In 1966, the Code was re-revised with

THE HAYS CODE

Before the Hays Code, when censorship was the responsibility of each state, the scissors were wielded in a very arbitrary manner. For example, a film called *Bobbed Hair* was cut by the state censors of Chicago in 1922 because of a scene in which a family man drew the curtains of his house. The Chicago censors felt that the audience might think the man had closed the curtains in order to kiss his wife!

With the introduction of the Hays Code, studios would pass their scripts to the Hays Office to check before starting filming. They didn't believe in spending money shooting scenes which the censors would subsequently cut. One of the many lines which failed to escape the censor's eagle eye was a typical piece of Mae West dialogue: 'Meet me at the pawnshop and I'll kiss you under the balls.'

If the Hays Code was backed by the all-powerful movie industry, the Catholic League of Decency had the might of the throne of Rome behind it. A 'C' or condemned rating from the League almost inevitably meant the failure of a film. When Tennessee Williams's story of rape and homosexuality, *A Streetcar Named*

Desire (1951), came up against the ultra-conservative League, it received the box-office kiss of death 'C' rating. This meant that millions of cinema-going Catholics would be instructed to boycott the film, while some theatres might ban it altogether. In order to salvage the film, a dozen cuts ordered by the League were made. One of the 12 cuts concerned the words '. . . on the mouth' following the statement, 'I would like to kiss you softly and sweetly . . .'

What the Hays Code said:

Sex

- The sanctity of the institution of marriage and the home shall be upheld. . . . Adultery and illicit sex, sometimes necessary plot material, must not be explicitly treated or justified, or presented attractively.

Scenes of Passion

- They should not be introduced except when they are definitely essential to the plot.

- Excessive and lustful kissing, lustful embraces, suggestive postures and gestures, are not to be shown.

Seduction or Rape

- They should never be more than suggested, and only when essential for the plot, and even then never shown by explicit method.

- They are never the proper subject for comedy.

- Sex perversion or any reference to it is forbidden.

- White slavery shall not be treated.

- Miscegenation (sex relationship between the white and black races) is forbidden.

- Sex hygiene and venereal diseases are not proper subjects for theatrical motion pictures.

- Scenes of actual childbirth, in fact or in silhouette, are never to be presented.

- Children's sex organs are never to be exposed.

Costume

- Complete nudity is never permitted.

- Undressing scenes should be avoided.

- Indecent or undue exposure is forbidden.

no positive prohibitions remaining.

While the Code was in effect, it had an enormous impact on Hollywood. Forties remakes of films of the late Twenties and early Thirties had to have scenes cut which had been allowable ten years earlier, because of the Hays Code. Hays became to Hollywood what Prohibition was to the American alcohol trade. Before 1934, Hollywood led Europe in the depiction of adult sexuality. But as the Hays Code began to take effect, directors focussed all their energy on ways of defying the restrictions.

—— PROHIBITED KISSES ——

One of the wiliest directors was Alfred Hitchcock. In *Notorious* (1946), he used every trick in the book to get round the Hays Code strictures on 'prolonged or excessive kissing'. The film stars Ingrid Bergman as the daughter of a Nazi spy who is asked by an American agent, Cary Grant (who also happens to be in love with her), to do some undercover work which involved her marrying a suspected Nazi. During the film there is a three-minute balcony kissing scene during which Grant and Bergman nibble at each other's lips, ears and neck while talking about the evening meal. This scene was deliberately devised by Hitchcock in an attempt to circumvent the Hays restrictions on prolonged kissing.

In the days when film-makers actually timed kisses by the second in order to stay within the rules, a straightforward sustained kiss would have provoked censorship. So Hitchcock, who dearly wanted to include a long, uninterrupted embrace, evaded the problem by making the kiss continual rather than continuous. Bergman and Grant begin their kiss on the balcony, and when the phone rings they move inside and across the room so that Grant can answer it. They resume their never really abandoned kiss, punctuated by Grant's virtually monosyllabic phone conversation. As Ingrid Bergman said, 'The censor couldn't cut it.'

Hitchcock felt that this kiss gave the public 'the great privilege of embracing Cary Grant and Ingrid Bergman together. It was a kind of

Director Hitchcock decided it was time to ring the changes in the Hays Code and persuaded Notorious *ladies' man, Cary Grant, to share his three-minute phone call with Ingrid Bergman to give the scene more bite.*

ménage à trois ... I felt that they should remain in an embrace and that we should join them. So when they got to the phone, the camera followed them, never leaving the close-up all the way right over to the door, all in one continuous shot ... Grant and Bergman told me they felt very awkward in that scene in *Notorious*. But I told them not to worry, it would look great on film and that's all that mattered. It's one of my most famous scenes.' (*The Life of Alfred Hitchcock*, Donald Spoto.) Publicity on the lengthy kiss certainly helped box-office takings.

——— ROSE-TINTED LENSES ———

Camera work was particularly important in filming screen kisses. Clever photography could mean the stars didn't even have to act; the passion would be suggested by the camera. An embrace in the film *A Place In The Sun* (1951) illustrates this perfectly. Elizabeth Taylor is a society girl, Montgomery Clift a factory worker with whom she falls in love. During a

Poor factory boy Montgomery Clift, on the look-out for A Place In The Sun, *ended up with more than just burnt fingers when rich girl Liz Taylor lit the fires of his passion.*

23

party, the two sneak off into the billiards room. As soon as the door closes, they kiss. That's all. They simply stand there holding the kiss while the camera does a 360 degree tracking shot around them, exploring the embrace. In the cinema, with the appropriate soundtrack, the effect was dynamite, extraordinarily sexual.

Hitchcock was a master of the 360 degree kiss. In his usual meticulous way, he went to great lengths to get the right shot. In *Vertigo* (1958), there are two particular scenes during which James Stewart and Kim Novak embrace: one in an hotel room, the other in a stable. Hitchcock had circular sets made of both places, and had the camera taken round each set in a 360-degree turn. During the hotel room kiss, the 360-degree shot was put on a screen on the back of the set. The actors stood on a small turntable and spun round slowly. As they went round and round, locked in a deep embrace, the screen behind them gave the appearance of going round with them, creating the impression of a deep, passionate kiss which went on and on . . .

Hitchcock always believed in bringing the camera as close as possible to screen lovers, in an effort to draw the audience into the kiss. He was trying to give the effect a viewer feels when he walks round Rodin's *The Kiss*, one of Hitchcock's favourite works of art. In *Vertigo*, Hitchcock was attempting to represent the lovers as Rodin had represented the lovers in *The Kiss* by focussing on the touch of the mouths, with the rest of the body only lightly touching.

CINDERELLA CENSORED

In Britain in the Thirties, producers were always battling with censorship. As Victor Saville reported: 'My friend, the story editor of Gaumont-British, and I worked out that if we were to obey every restriction set up by the British Board of Film censors . . . you wouldn't be able to make Cinderella.'

——— THE FADE-OUT ———

With censorship severely restricting sexual activity, a passionate kiss between a man and a woman was Hollywood's most explicit depiction

Kim Novak suffers a touch of Vertigo *as she looks up at lanky hero James Stewart, now in a spin because he's not only lost his head for heights but he's also lost the girl he loved.*

of sexual urges. That doesn't mean to say that the heroines of the Thirties and Forties weren't sexually active. Long kisses, mostly out of doors (if the censors glimpsed a bed during a love scene, the scissors would almost certainly be wielded), followed by the actors disappearing from the camera's view and a slow fade-out told the audience exactly what the position was. Sex was all right in its place – beyond the camera's view.

The audience were eager conspirators in the plot to hoodwink the censors. Thus in *Humoresque* (1946), they know that when Joan Crawford and John Garfield, after fencing verbally for half the picture, go riding together they're not just out for the exercise. Predictably, Crawford takes a tumble, which gives Garfield the chance to join her on the ground. As they go into the kiss, the camera focusses on them for a short while before they drop down out of sight and the camera remains, focussed on the beautiful seashore in the background . . . then fades out . . .

After a tumble in the grass, inexpert horsewoman Joan Crawford accepts a helping hand from John Garfield while he works out whether her injuries merit a kiss of life. Just as the director calls, 'Cut', he makes up his mind and the camera catches the beginning of the clinch before they fade out of sight.

DRAMATIC DEVICES

Just as in the Twenties, kissing wasn't always a signal for sex. It was used as a dramatic device, often to suggest feelings which couldn't be put across in words. Gangsters' molls came in for a lot of dramatic kissing. A favourite ploy of the gun-crazed hoodlum was to let the woman give him the come-on, then as her lips parted in a kiss, he would use his thumb to smear her lipstick down her lower lip and chin. Practised by James Cagney and Humphrey Bogart, this was the ultimate gesture of contempt, the signal to the audience that she was worthless, cheap. In one gesture, it destroyed the woman's looks, her sexuality and her confidence.

REVILED KISSES

While thousands of women around the world would have given anything for just one kiss with their favourite screen hero, there were some actresses who hated every second of their celluloid love scenes. Although *Gone With The Wind* (1939) made her famous, Vivien Leigh loathed the film-making and the love-making. As

27

Rhett Butler, Clark Gable may have had a silver tongue: 'Here's a soldier of the South who loves you, Scarlett, wants to feel your arms around him, wants to carry the memory of your kisses into battle with him. Never mind about loving me. You're a women sending a soldier to his death with a beautiful memory. Scarlett, kiss me. Kiss me once' – but as a flesh and blood screen idol, Gable's false teeth and whisky-laden breath made her shudder with distaste. (She wasn't the first actress to be put off by Gable's falsies. A young actress who was unaware of the true state of Gable's dentures, was leaving the set one day after an intimate scene with the star when she spotted him washing his false teeth in the sink outside the dressing-room.)

While Vivien Leigh was repulsed by Gable's touch, off-screen she and Laurence Olivier, with whom she

The filming of Gone With The Wind *marked Vivien Leigh's first big break when she captured the most sought-after role in screen history, Scarlett O'Hara. She had just fallen in love with the more established and already married Laurence Olivier. He took a role on Broadway while she filmed* Gone With The Wind *so that they could be together occasionally. Off-screen her love life had never been better; on screen, she complained of Gable's bad breath and false teeth.*

was having a passionate affair, couldn't keep their hands off each other. As Sunny, Vivien's secretary and companion during the filming, said: 'He was always kissing her. Holding her hand. Or his arm around her shoulder. She was most responsive. They were more like teenage lovers than two adults who had been married before and each had a child.'

In his early films, Gable's enthusiastic kisses couldn't be faulted, though his technique was rare, medium rare in fact. Gable confessed that in love scenes with his female co-stars, he invariably thought of a steak. He acquired this odd tech-

LIP SYNCH

Actress Cybill Shepherd reports that some of her on-screen lovers were dud smoochers. She refuses to kiss and tell, however, preferring to heap praise on one or two specially chosen leading men. She says that she and Gregory Harrison, her co-star in the film. *Seduced*, are in lip synch. 'It's fun doing love scenes with Gregory. He's not only a fine actor but also a very good kisser. I wish I could say that about all my leading men.'

29

nique when confronted with the terrifying prospect of playing opposite Norma Shearer, his boss, Irving Thalberg's wife, in *A Free Soul* (1931). Miss Shearer played the wild, reckless daughter of a famous attorney (Lionel Barrymore) who had become a drunk. Gable, in one of his first big screen roles, played a gambler with whom she becomes infatuated.

Lionel Barrymore tells of strolling on the set one day to watch this new young actor and seeing Gable wolfishly hugging and kissing Shearer. He was amazed at Gable's nonchalance: when Gable spotted Barrymore, he just raised his arm but not his lips. In fact, Gable was terrified, but he knew he had to pass this test to make it as an actor. Earlier, he'd been admonished by the director for not looking at Miss Shearer with enough longing during their love scenes. Long afterwards, Gable explained how he rectified this. 'When I looked at Norma, I didn't think of her at all but of a thick, juicy steak. Longing for a steak and longing for a woman must make a guy look the same way because the director said: "That's great, kid!"'

As Gable got older, however, his longing for a steak diminished. One critic said of the 54-year-old's love scenes with Lana Turner in *Betrayed* (1954): 'Clark Gable kissed Lana Turner like a husband with a hangover.'

SCREEN AFFAIRS

If kissing a co-star you hated wasn't much fun, kissing someone you fancied was often a much more alarming proposition. The consequences of screen affairs lingered on long after the set had been dismantled and the film crew had dispersed. Many a marriage foundered as picture partners picked up off screen where they had left off on it.

Probably the most famous screen liaison was that between Elizabeth Taylor and Richard Burton, who met while shooting *Cleopatra* in 1963 in

Clark Gable proves the studio didn't make a big mis-steak when it gave him the lead role in A Free Soul, *playing opposite Norma Shearer, studio boss Irving Thalberg's wife. When she failed to excite the requisite response during their love scenes, Gable conjured up a big juicy steak to increase his appetite, winning the approval of the director and a new career as a screen heart-throb.*

Italy. Their love-making scenes were the talk of Rome and before filming had finished, each of their respective partners had left the city in a huff.

One of the most poignant and ultimately successful screen romances was that between the 43-year-old Hollywood veteran, Humphrey Bogart, and the 20-year-old newcomer, Lauren Bacall. In *To Have and Have Not* (1944), their first film together, the liberated Bacall not only made the first moves but was also brash enough to criticise her lover's kissing style as well. After their first kiss, initiated by her, she unselfconsciously tells him: 'It's even better if you help.' Later in the film she ventures another opinion on Bogart's talents. 'I like that, except for the beard. Why don't you shave and we'll try that again.'

Errol Flynn was notorious for flirting outrageously on screen – although he saved his most passionate scenes for the court room. (He successfully defended at least two accusations of

Burton holds Taylor at arm's length in a short-lived attempt to stave off the inevitable. While Cleopatra detained Anthony in Egypt, keeping him away from his senatorial duties, off-screen both Taylor and Burton abandoned their marital obligations, begetting an on-off romance spanning two marriages over two decades.

rape and countless paternity suits.) In the Thirties, Flynn teamed up with Olivia de Havilland for a string of costume dramas ranging from *Captain Blood* (1935) to *Robin Hood* (1938). It was public knowledge around the film studio that de Havilland carried a torch for Flynn. Knowing Flynn's reputation, Jack Warner of Warner Brothers warned him to be nice to her.

Flynn was only predictable in that he could be guaranteed to do the opposite of what he had been asked. In Robin Hood, he teased his way through a series of reshoots, kissing Miss de Havilland more ardently each time in the sure knowledge that there would have to be yet another retake because their embraces wouldn't get through the Hays Office.

At least this film cured Miss de Havilland of her crush: she grew progressively more annoyed by Flynn's vanity during their love scenes. Since his wife, Lili Damita, had told him he

The screen kiss that began an off-screen partnership that lasted until the tragic death of Bogart in 1958. 20-year-old 'Betty' Bacall captivated the twice-married, heavy-drinking middle-aged star, when they appeared together for the first time in To Have and Have Not.

Robin Hood – *the film that cured Olivia de Havilland of her crush for the much-married screen Lothario Errol Flynn. Told by his wife that in lovers' close-ups, his eyes looked too small, he concentrated his attention on de Havilland's forehead in order to make them look bigger.*

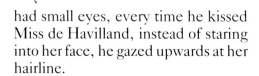

had small eyes, every time he kissed Miss de Havilland, instead of staring into her face, he gazed upwards at her hairline.

SCREEN HEROINES

While there was no equivalent to screen heart throbs like Errol Flynn and Clark Gable among the ranks of the female stars, actresses too suffered from sexual typecasting. It was only as they got older that the range of parts they were offered widened. Marlene Dietrich, for example, was seen as mysterious and erotic, but not passionate, while under the direction of her long-time mentor, Von Sternberg – although in *Morocco* in 1930 she shocked the public when, dressed in drag, she kissed another girl on the mouth.

Having broken free of Von Sternberg, though, she established a reputation within the industry as a 'hard kisser'. When, in 1936, she began making films in England for Alexander Korda, he received a cable from Wally Westmore, the Hollywood make-up expert, saying: 'For Heaven's sake, watch her make-up. She needs a new mouth after every kiss. This Dietrich has become the

SCREEN KISSAHOLICS

Who were our greatest screen kissers? Whose lips, pressed against another's on celluloid, sent the audience's pulse rate soaring? Clark Gable? No, co-stars complained of his bad breath and, worse, false teeth, while directors criticised his lack of ardour. Errol Flynn, notorious off-screen leading figure in many a court case? No, anxiety about his small, beady eyes prevented him from giving vent to his screen passions. Greta Garbo? Only on the occasions when her screen lover also happened to be her choice in real life, too. Jane Russell (right in *His Kind Of Woman* with Robert Mitchum.) Not if kissing interfered with gum chewing. (She would stick the gum up her co-star's nose in the kissing scenes.)

Perhaps the prize for the greatest screen kiss ought to go to the actress whose name is down in the records books for two extraordinary feats, not totally unconnected with one another. Not only is she one half of the longest-ever screen kissing partnership – clocking up a steamy 185-second kiss with Regis Toomey in *You're In The Army Now* (1941) – she also happens to be Ronald Reagan's first wife. Could Jane Wyman be responsible for the kissaholic the President has become?

When Joan Crawford married her first husband, Douglas Fairbanks Jnr, in 1929, she bought a house which had rustic stepping stones across the front lawn, leading up to the hall door with its knocker sculpted in the shape of two heads, male and female, their lips pressed together in a kiss.

hardest kisser in movies.'

In the Thirties, Joan Crawford had a reputation for having affairs with her leading men – Clark Gable when she was still married to Douglas Fairbanks Jnr., and later with Franchot Tone in *Dancing Lady* (1933). Ironically, although it was Clark Gable, the star of the film, who won her heart on screen, it was Tone, with whom she shares an underwater kissing scene, whom she married two years later.

In Dancing Lady. *Joan Crawford was taken in by the smooth-talking, wealthy Franchot Tone, until she discovered that beneath co-star Clark Gable's tough exterior beat a heart of gold. Joan Crawford and Franchot Tone, who married two years after making this film, shared an underwater kissing sequence which raised the water temperature and caused quite a few surface bubbles.*

Despite her reputation, when Crawford starred opposite Michael Wilding in *Torch Song* (1953), she not only didn't have an affair with him, she never opened her mouth to him off the set. The first scene they played together (he was a blind pianist, she a successful but bitchy singer) was also the last scene of the film – predictably The Kiss. After the shot was in the can, Wilding quipped that it was the first time he had kissed a woman before they were introduced.

Crawford was certainly no screen virgin, unlike Doris Day whose reputation as the golden girl next door dogged her film career. But even the supposedly chaste Miss Day was not without her admirers. James Garner, who starred with her in *Thrill Of It All* (1963) said of their love scenes: 'The cliché thing to say about a movie love scene is that it's just a mechanical thing – you sit in front of the camera and kiss the girl and the whistle blows and you go home and never give it another thought. Well, that's useful

In Torch Song Michael Wilding failed to light any fires in Ms Crawford's notoriously combustible heart, while she preferred to give him the silent treatment, communicating in sign language on screen and refusing to speak a word to him off.

40

propaganda for the wives at home. ("Now, honey, how could there be anything going on between us when there's 100 grips and electricians and cameramen around us?"). But the fact of the matter is that with Doris, 100 grips or not, there was always something there and I must admit that if I had not been married, I would have tried to carry forward after hours where we left off on the sound stage.' (*Doris Day, Her Own Story*, A. E. Hotchner.)

Another ice goddess, Grace Kelly, thawed considerably during her screen career. At drama school in New York, she had to be taught how to kiss by Worthington Myler, a TV producer and director. 'She was so shy. She stood too far away and had to be taught how to lean forward,' he said.

Hitchcock used this shyness to great effect in *To Catch A Thief* (1955). He placed the camera in such a way that the first shots of Kelly were in

In The Thrill Of It All, *James Garner certainly doesn't look too thrilled when Doris Day tells him she really can't see him that night because she's just washed her hair. As a doctor specialising in 'women's problems', Mr Garner's medical expertise is no help at all in solving his own problems when Day, his hitherto stay-at-home wife, takes on a new and successful career as an advertising model.*

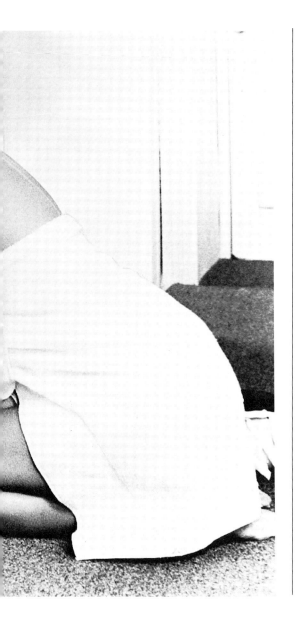

In What's Up Doc, *Ryan O'Neal baulks at taking off his necktie and leaving his jugular defenceless to dotty Barbra Streisand's machinations.*

profile with her showing little expression. When she suddenly turns in the doorway of her room and kisses Cary Grant, the impact is enormous. The cool blonde bowls him, and the audience, over.

Grace Kelly nearly didn't make it to the set of *To Catch A Thief*. Her previous film, *Green Fire* (1954), in which she starred with Stewart Granger, had over-run its schedule. In *Green Fire*, Grace and Granger had several love scenes. As Granger says, 'Grace had one problem: her behind. For me, it was the most delicious behind imaginable, but it did stick out a bit and she was very self-conscious about it. Our last scene was played in a torrential downpour and when the final kiss came, we were both soaking wet, which accentuated that fabulous behind. To save her

NO CARRY ON

Actress Melanie Griffith was dismissed from Brian de Palma's 1976 film *Carrie* because she wouldn't kiss an actor she didn't know.

Ice goddess, Grace Kelly, thaws quickly under the melting embrace of retired cat burglar, Cary Grant, in To Catch A Thief *(left).*

Fired with enthusiasm for her next film with Hitchcock, To Catch A Thief, Kelly *nearly didn't make it in time, when filming on* Green Fire *with Stewart Granger (right) was held up.*

embarrassment, I covered it with both hands. She was so delighted at finishing the film (in order to start work on *To Catch A Thief*) that she didn't object, but if you look closely at that kiss, you'll see Grace give a start as two eager hands take hold.' (*Sparks Fly Upward*, Granger.)

—— HALITOSIS AND WORSE ——

Male co-stars have their own horror stories of tortuous love scenes with actresses suffering from halitosis. Actors suffered from the misguided notion that they could turn it on any time, any place ... But as Granger relates, love scenes weren't always the picnic they appeared. 'I think any leading actor will agree that there's nothing romantic or sexy about kissing all those fabulous mouths. Personally, I don't like kissing in public, and on a film set there are always about 60 bored faces looking on. Then there's the positioning. When you're kissing someone you really fancy, you're not concerned with where the noses go and what's the best angle of the half face exposed to the cameras. You're not concerned with mucking up her make-up which, you are warned, will take half an hour to repair. Then I've always found it difficult to make love at nine o'clock in the morning. After a few belts in the evening because the day's work is almost over it's easier to get in the mood, but having to pick up the same scene the next morning and show the same enthusiasm takes more acting ability than I possess.

'Many of my films were in costume and naturally you didn't have many duplicated because of the expense. It's hot working under the lights and you sweat. After a few weeks, the costumes become high and although dried and disinfected by the wardrobe department each night, it only took a few hours under the lights for them to start ponging again.

'Then there's halitosis. Not everyone has a breath like new-mown hay. When you're nervous in a scene, it often affects your stomach which in turn affects your breath. I must have acted with many nervous actresses. One, I remember, was the most beautiful, enchanting creature it was possible to imagine, but she

Although Tony Curtis likened his love scenes with Marilyn Monroe in Some Like It Hot *to 'kissing Hitler', many critics claim it was one of his best films.*

had the breath of a lion. Playing love scenes with her was torture, especially the ones where you breathe your passion for each other with your mouths inches apart so that you can both be in the lens at the same time. I used to take a deep breath and try to play the whole scene without inhaling. I made three films with that lady and it was good for my breath control.

'I'm sure actresses had the same experience with some of their leading men. I would gargle and try to make sure I offended as little as possible, but I've been told that not all actors were so thoughtful.'

Joan Collins never got the chance to find out whether her most famous co-star, Richard Burton, was as thoughtful – and as orally hygienic – as Granger. In a part which was head-lined at the time as a monumental piece of miscasting, she played a nun shipwrecked on a desert island with three men. Roberto Rossellini, the director of the film, *Sea Wife* (1957), had demanded Joan for the role against great opposition.

Rossellini had been given a free hand in the film – except for one thing. Fox Studios insisted that Burton and Collins were not to kiss on screen. Fox was afraid that an illicit kiss would enrage the Catholic women's groups of America. So while Rossellini worked on Fox to persuade them to change their minds, the screenwriter worked on two different scripts – one with the kiss and one without. While cast and crew sat soaking up the sun and the local hooch on a Jamaican beach waiting for the final script decision, back in Hollywood furious arguments raged. Fox refused to approve the script with the kiss, so Rossellini resigned and another director, Bob McNaughton, took over the film.

—————— *FORBIDDEN AREAS* ——————

The Hays Code certainly inhibited the depiction of explicit sex in the cinema. The areas of oral exploration were restricted to the face, neck and shoulders – body kissing was definitely taboo. But the war had a tremendous effect on the moral climate, which was reflected in the

Ditched on a desert island with only 3 men for company, novice nun Joan Collins, in Sea Wife, *shuns the call of the flesh and turns her back on founding a dynasty with Richard Burton. Back in Hollywood, Fox studio executives heaved a giant sigh of relief that a moral outcry from the Catholic League of Decency had been averted.*

Carried away by waves of salty passion, this briny embrace in From Here To Eternity *certainly put new life in the careers of Burt Lancaster and Deborah Kerr. But film censors were afraid this salacious scene would prove to be just a short step from here to maternity for aroused audiences. If the censors had had their way, the most famous beach scene on celluloid would have looked very different indeed. Director Fred Zinnemann was threatened with an adults-only rating, which would have seriously damaged the film's distribution prospects, unless the scene was re-shot with one of the empassioned stars wearing a beach robe. When he refused to comply, the censors gave way and cinema's most memorable kiss went ahead.*

cinema. The film that signalled the great change in love-making mores was *The Outlaw* (1943), starring sex queen, Jane Russell. This low-budget Western made by the legendary millionaire, Howard Hughes, was shot at the beginning of the Forties but was held up by the Hays Office not because the camera took every opportunity to focus on Russell's most prominent assets, but because of one scene which they considered went beyond the sexual pale.

In this scene, Russell learns that her cowboy lover is dying of pneumonia, so she undresses, puts on a modest nightie and climbs into bed to keep him warm. Years passed with Hughes defiantly refusing to cut the offending scene and the Hays Office equally adamantly refusing to pass it. Eventually, in 1950, the film was released nationally and was a great success, despite its lack of a seal of approval.

Hughes's victory showed other directors that if they were prepared to fight, they could stand up against the

Check mate for bored millionaire Steve McQueen and slick insurance investigator Faye Dunaway in The Thomas Crown Affair. *This close-up comes a close second to the longest-ever screen kiss and marked the end of a long chess game.*

Hays Office – and win. In 1953, Otto Preminger's *The Moon is Blue* (1953), the story of a virgin who looked forward to her seduction, was also successfully released without a seal. Starring David Niven, William Holden and Maggie Mcnamara, it was sentences like, 'Men are usually so bored with virgins. I'm glad you're not.' which outraged the censors.

The writing was on the wall for the Hays Code, particularly when its objections to the famous beach love scene in *From Here To Eternity* (1953) were also ignored. The film censor, a Mr Breen, demanded '. . . either Karen [Deborah Kerr] or Warden [Burt Lancaster] put on a beach robe or some other type of clothing before they go into their embrace.' Like Hughes and Preminger, director Fred Zinemann refused, and the film was a phenomenal success.

The end of the Fifties and beginning of the Sixties coincided with a social, cultural and artistic revolution which saw the introduction of a new kind of freedom in the cinema. Films like *Room At The Top* (1958), which was released without a seal, and the *Thomas Crown Affair* (1968), in which Steve McQueen and Faye Dunaway play a symbolic chess game – all wet

55

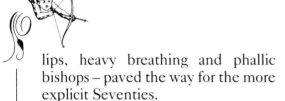

lips, heavy breathing and phallic bishops – paved the way for the more explicit Seventies.

Today, adherence to any cinematic moral code is only skin deep. Kisses are no longer chastely confined to the upper region of the body but planted every which way but one . . . and genital kissing will probably soon be brought out of the shadows of the Eighties discreet fade-out.

At a time when film-stars-turned-president-of-the-United-States grab every opportunity to smooch with their leading lady; when princes no longer have to go through the frog stage to be kissed by princesses; and when osculation is practised by the highest and the lowest in the land as an everyday form of greeting, the art of screen kissing is no longer a mouth-watering prospect for a climax-hungry audience.

Perhaps the last words ought to be left to veteran film star and comedian Bob Hope: 'They are doing things on the screen now that I wouldn't do in bed. If I could.'

Richard Gere takes a lucky dip while a Breathless *Valerie Kaprisky pretends she's really in need of mouth to mouth resuscitation. Still, if a girl needs a cold bath before kissing you as well as after, you know you're on the right track.*

SOCIAL KISSING

Kissing today has come out of the bedroom and into the street. Everybody's doing it: actors and actresses, politicians and society hostesses, models and chat show hosts, churchgoers and social climbers, fathers and babies, men and women – even the Royal Family. Kissing has replaced the handshake as the natural salutation and greeting.

The practice of giving your host or hostess some lip has been like a kiss of life to the social scene. Now, in restaurants, offices and even on street corners, members of both sexes can be seen ducking and weaving in an attempt to deliver the new couth kiss in the appropriate manner.

A far cry from its sex-based sister, the social kiss can signal hello, goodbye, congratulations – or simply hide your embarrassment while you hunt

The Queen Mother (below) being treated to a bit of olde world chivalry. In this case, though the spirit is willing, the technique is all wrong. One hand should be used to draw the lady's hand gently towards the lips which should hover discreetly rather than land. All the great masters operate from the bended knee.

Princess Diana (right), on a royal tour in Norway, keeps her distance, obviously unaware that the cold would kill off most of the 250 bacteria people exchange when they kiss.

your memory for a name to put to the cheek. And unlike the passionate clinch, the salutary kiss involves little or no bodily contact. Apart from the right hand, which rests in a chaste manner on the left forearm of the person being greeted, the only contact is made by the lips. Pursed lips are aimed somewhere between the

59

top of the cheekbone and the ear – though pressing lips too close to the ear, one of the body's erogenous zones, is a definite breach of social manners.

The social kiss should never be practised after taking strenuous exercise: a stream of hot air whistling past your partner's ear is considered very suggestive indeed and not quite in keeping with the platonic tone of the greeting. And lips must always be dry; a moist mouthful ranks as one of the greatest social blunders.

Because cheek-to-cheek kissing means that for a second or two, both parties are beyond each other's view, a signal is imperative to mark the end of the kiss. By making a smacking noise as you kiss, both of you can then withdraw safely, knowing your social obligations have been fulfilled. Moreover, the noise warns others in the vicinity that your brief tête-à-tête is not a cover-up for a blazing affair.

There's a definite pecking order when it comes to social kissing. For men, duty calls when their wife, girlfriend, fiancé, live-in lover, mother, granny, or favourite aunt are around. Sisters, however, only merit a kiss in a crowd, such as at parties or family celebrations. On the whole,

British men tend not to kiss their own sex – unless they're actors, senior politicians or on the sports field. Women, however, are allowed free rein: they can kiss girlfriends, men friends, parents, parents-in-law, colleagues – and even the Prince of Wales. But kisses between females is subject to Darwin's law: it's always the stronger of the two who initiates the embrace. Female business associates kiss both hello and good-bye – unless their meeting involved more than fifty percent business discussions.

Traditionally, the British have embraced with an encounter of the single cheek to cheek kind. But recently, we've been adopting Gallic mannerisms and going for the double cheek lock. Apeing the casual sophistication of the Parisians, double kissers always aim for the left cheek first followed by the right. Trendier Brits, especially among the County set, go one better and slip in another to the left just as their partner thinks they've finished.

If you've known someone of the

Princess Margaret takes this opportunity to pass a discreet communication to her sister at the Chelsea Flower Show.

opposite sex for years, perhaps even indulged in a light flirtation from time to time, you're allowed to greet them with a kiss on the lips. But lip pressure must be minimal and of short duration, otherwise you're likely to exchange semiochemicals (see page 77) and wreak havoc on your platonic relationship.

The way you kiss says as much about you as the clothes you wear. Male actors kiss each other on the cheek, male musicians embrace, grasping each other at the elbow and squeezing gently; female members of the Royal Family aim for the cheek but miss, and end up brushing the air instead of ruining the hair; society hostesses kiss with their head up and eyes wide open in case someone higher up the social scale arrives; politicians kiss you and grasp your hand at the same time so they use it to propel themselves forward to the next person in case of awkward questions; guests at the same party are treated to one peck only, while the host receives a double embrace.

— THE ORAL PECKING ORDER —

There are other types of kiss besides the kiss of salutation. Babies are kissed on the top of the head. Children's injuries are kissed 'to make them better', dice are kissed for luck, religious relics are kissed with reverence, brides are kissed by the best man, bishops' rings are kissed as a sign of respect, frogs are kissed and turn into princes, princesses are kissed and live happily ever after.

Kissing on the lips, however, dates back to Roman times when anxious husbands explored their wives' lips to find out if they'd been drinking during the day. In fact, the Romans were so keen on the practice that they had three words for it: osculum – meaning the kiss to the cheek between friends; basium – the kiss on the lips, and suavium – the lover's kiss. But Emperor Tiberius banned the practice when lip sores became endemic throughout the population.

Even in ancient times, kissing had a social pecking order. Then, two equals kissed each other on the cheek at equal body height. Kisses between those of unequal status, however,

To the Romans go the honour of introducing the kiss to modern civilization. A nation to whom the words veni, vidi, vici *(I came, I saw, I conquered) were a familiar victory chant, was also well endowed with soldiers who knew their duty was to toe the line by laying down their arms before a lady of Patrician birth and reverently kissing her feet.*

had to be performed at a level low enough to signify that status. Thus, the lowliest was obliged to kiss the foot of his superior – except in the case of prisoners who were deemed so inferior that they weren't even allowed a foothold, but had to be content with pressing their lips to the ground next to their superior's foot. (Hence the expression 'kiss the dirt'.)

As the level of superiority rose, so did the kisses. Next up in the pecking order was allowed to kiss the hem of his superior's garment; further up again, the kisser aimed for the knee. A bishop, for instance, was allowed to kiss the Pope's knee whereas a layperson only got as far as the right shoe. The modern-day Pope sometimes does the kissing himself, but in his case on the head. (Right: The Pope kissing the Canadian head of state.)

Almost until modern times, the kiss was the normal form of greeting between men as well as between men and women. In Persia, men of equal rank kissed each other on the mouth while men of unequal status kissed on the cheek. In most countries, however, lip to cheek kissing was the normal practise between equals.

PUTTING THE SQUEEZE ON

The practice of kissing the pope's shoe began in the 8th century when a misguided lady squeezed the hand of His Holiness. The affectionate tug so shocked the pope with lascivious thoughts that he had his hand cut off. Henceforth it was practice to kiss the foot instead.

KISSING GOES OUT OF FASHION

In medieval England, knights behaved pretty much as do footballers today, kissing and hugging each other on the jousting field. It was only at the beginning of the eighteenth century that the non-sexual kiss as a greeting went out of fashion, particularly in the new, large industrialised towns where people were less likely to know each other. In the country, kissing as a greeting still continued for some time.

In America, Puritan communities in New England made it a crime to join lips with one's wife on the Sabbath. One clever follower, less fanatical than the rest, tried to get round the law by kissing another man's wife on Sunday. Unfortunately, his ruse was spotted by a 'sin snooper' and he was severely punished.

In Russia, after the Bolshevik Revolution in 1917, some of the more fanatical revolutionaries denounced kissing as a decadent bourgeois habit. Some tyrannical local commisars tried to suppress the practice altogether. But their task proved so difficult that very soon the Bolsheviks 'discovered' that the custom predated the capitalist era and osculation resumed its normal course.

In Italy during the Thirties and Forties, Mussolini outlawed public kissing as unseemly – except in railway stations. With so many young lovers taking leave of each other as men left for the front, anyone who wished to circumvent the law would just turn up at the local station and indulge in protracted leave-taking.

Although kissing as a greeting declined in popularity, men would still kiss a lady's hand in welcome. Etiquette dictated that the lady in question profer her hand first which the gentleman would then take in his own hand before gently pressing his lips to it. As this action became more stylised, the kissing element declined in importance to the point where the man's puckered lips would simply kiss the air just above the lady's hand. Later, kissing was dropped in favour of a polite bow.

THE BUNDLING BOARD

Kissing has not always met with parental approval, but strange things have happened . . .

At the turn of the century, when courting was a matter of great family

65

concern, kissing was an integral part of parents' plans for their offspring. So much so that the bedroom, not the living room, was considered the best place for a couple to engage in kissing.

The courting couple would meet in the girl's family house where they would have a meal together. At bedtime, the mother took a bundling sack from her old chest and the father brought down the bundling board from the attic. Stepping into the sack, the girl would then be tied in by her mother, and tucked into her own bed next to her partner-to-be. The bundling board would then be placed between them and fastened firmly to the foot and head of the bed. When the parents left, the young couple would lie in the dark stealing kisses over the top of the bundling board. In the morning, if the kissing had been enjoyable, they would usually announce their impending marriage.

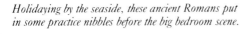

Holidaying by the seaside, these ancient Romans put in some practice nibbles before the big bedroom scene.

THE KISSING BOUGH

Kissing has always played a large part in home life. Before the days of paper decorations, the Kissing Bough was a prominent feature of most people's homes at Yuletide. A garland of greenery, the Kissing Bough hung from the middle of the ceiling in the living-room. Shaped like a double hooped garland or gown, it had candles, apples, rosettes of coloured paper and ornaments of various kinds hanging from it. Sometimes, small presents were suspended from it at the ends of long ribbon streamers. But the most important item was the bunch of mistletoe in the centre. In some districts, where the plant was scarce, the bunch was omitted and the Bough itself was called the mistletoe.

The candles were ceremoniously lit on Christmas Eve and every consecutive night during the twelve days of Christmas. Throughout the festive season, the Kissing Bough was the centre of the family's celebrations, under which carols were sung, games played and kisses exchanged. But in the middle of the last century, the Kissing Bough was replaced by the Christmas tree, which now takes

Cousin Charles puts his neck out and risks a rebuff from his fair relative despite the fact that the hanging bough of mistletoe shows custom is on his side.

pride of place in the Yuletide festivities.

Kissing under the mistletoe seems to be an entirely English custom, only found in other countries when they have been settled by English immigrants. Its long-lived popularity may be partly due to the fact that until the early 17th century the English were much given to kissing as a form of greeting. Foreign visitors noted with surprise – and pleasure – how freely men and women kissed each other on meeting and parting and how even strangers, on their first introduction into a family, were permitted, and even expected, to kiss the host's wife and daughters on their lips. Erasmus, writing from London to a friend in Rotterdam back in the sixteenth century, noted: 'There is, besides, a custom which it would be impossible to praise too much. Wherever you go, everyone welcomes you with a kiss, and the same on bidding farewell. You call again, when there is more kissing . . . in short, turn where you will, there are kisses, kisses everywhere.'

The Festive Season provided notable excuses for kissing. In Scotland, kissing for luck during Hogmanay was a general custom for centuries. Every male was permitted to salute young women of his acquaintance in the early hours of the New Year. 'The young women walk about the streets (of Edinburgh) without fear,' wrote an observer in 1857, 'as nobody thinks of interfering with them in the way of salutation till the town clock warns the approach of twelve. Within a few minutes of that hour, young women of all ranks may be seen creeping along close to the wall, thinking to gain their houses without being discovered; young men may also be seen moving after them, only waiting for the warning clock in order to make the salute which cannot be rejected.'

Even a lady who passes in a sedan chair or a carriage submits with the best grace she can to pay the forfeit she has incurred.

ROYAL KISSES

Even before Prince Charles and Princess Diana enthralled a nation with their wedding day balcony kiss, the royal kiss has been an object of concern to newspapers around the world. And until Diana appeared on the marital scene, it was always Charles at the centre of a kissing controversy.

Buckingham Palace doesn't actually veto public kissing of the royal family, but it's widely understood that a handshake, curtsey or bow is a more proper form of greeting. On a royal tour of Australia, however, a kiss chasing population showed the British public how to develop the royal kissing habit. British crowds may have given the heir to the throne

69

Charles and Diana entranced the world with the first public kiss only hours after their fairytale wedding in St. Paul's Cathedral in July 1981. The most famous royal kiss was watched by millions of people all over the world, as well as thousands who had flocked to Buckingham Palace to see the royal pair. This spontaneous kiss belied the image of the archetypal Englishman and his stiff upper lip. It also revealed that in those days, Charles and Diana still had a lot to learn: the fact that they've both got their eyes open indicated it's hard for them to relax and give in to the enchantment of the kiss.

STOLEN KISSES

In 1979, Prince Charles visited Nottingham where he was set upon by three young girls intent on stealing a kiss. Afterwards he said, 'One of them kissed me particularly aggressively – which gave me enormous pleasure.'

a bruised hand, but he almost ended up with bruised lips after his 1977 tour down under.

The Australians proved to be determined and resourceful kiss chasers, refusing to be put off by bodyguards or protocol. One Australian lady was even cheeky enough to make a second attempt on the Prince. During the 1977 tour, Sylvia Cresnar broke through the security barriers at Adelaide airport and hurled herself at him before stealing a kiss and being led away. Four years

Lydia Grombele unleashes an Antipodean smacker on a politely restrained Prince Charles. One suspects that were not half of Sydney present, Prince Charles may have been tempted to take his other arm from behind his back to deal firmly and properly with this sensual, full-lipped temptress. Sadly, iron self-discipline prevailed and he managed to avert his eyes from her barely-covered cleavage.

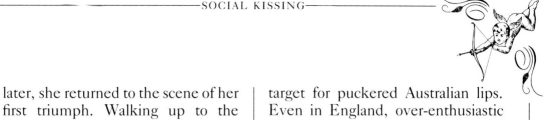

later, she returned to the scene of her first triumph. Walking up to the Prince, she asked if he remembered her. Prince Charles may have been kissed by thousands of lips since 1977, but he gallantly replied in the affirmative, whereupon she threw her arms around him and kissed him on the lips.

The British, notoriously mingy with their kisses, learnt a few lessons from the Australians and took to addressing the prince on more intimate terms during his walkabouts. Historically, the servants of great leaders kissed hands, garments and even the floor, while the mouth to mouth kiss denoted equal status. The British crowd didn't go quite as far as claiming equal status but at least they kissed at a level of equal height. Psychologists believe the craze for kissing the Prince has its roots in the primitive belief that glory will rub off. But it's not only the royal men who suffer from the kiss chase syndrome. Back in Australia again in 1983, the female half of the royal couple became the number one

A chap used to express fondness for his frère with a good old slap on the back. Here, the royal princes seem to have discovered some French blood.

target for puckered Australian lips. Even in England, over-enthusiastic admirers let their enthusiasm get the better of protocol. Still, at least the Princess cannot have been as shocked as the Queen Mother when pecked on the cheek by former President Jimmy Carter. A widow since 1952, the Queen Mother is said to have commented with no great pleasure, 'This is the first man who has kissed me since my husband.'

Younger members of the royal family have also come in for their share of the kiss chase. Unfortunately, Prince Andrew's brushes with lips have mostly been of the kiss and tell variety, though one tell-tale, former girlfriend Sandi Jones, did reveal that he was 'a great kisser'.

But it's the youngest member of the royal family, Prince Edward, whose kisses have made the greatest impact. While a first-year student at Jesus College, Cambridge, Edward was greeted with a kiss by his eldest brother, much to the consternation of the British press. The French may do it, so may the Greeks, the Argentines, the Sikhs and the Russians but unless on a football field, men rarely do it to each other – until the royal princes showed the way.

73

SEXUAL KISSING

To a nation reared on the steamy passion of celluloid kisses, kissing lessons began with the first trip to the cinema. But the screen's kissing curriculum left a lot to be desired. Ingrid Bergman's naïve admission to Gary Cooper in *For Whom The Bell Tolls* (1943) – 'I don't know how to kiss or I would kiss you. Where do the noses go?' – was echoed in many a teenage breast at the time. The problem with two-dimensional screen heroes and heroines was perspective: the camera rarely got close enough to reveal what happened when their mouths met. Were their lips parted? Their mouths open? Did they use their tongues? To a country like America, where the underwear industry practically collapsed when Clark Gable shed his vest on film, answers to questions like this were imperative to a happy sex life. While the censors made sure screen kisses were about as erotic as kissing your granny, the camera ensured that any straying away from the strictures of the Hays Code was a secret kept strictly between the Thespians concerned.

Those who swooned when Bergman and Bogart embraced in Casablanca, who cried when Leslie Howard pressed one last kiss to a dying Olivia de Havilland's lips in *Gone With the Wind*, found that in real life, mouths were warm and wet, hard and overpowering, pursed or parted.

Social kisses, which in recent years have crossed the formality barriers, proved to be no nursery school for anyone looking to a kiss to clinch a relationship. Kisses may be one step up from handshakes in the social pecking order, but when it came to dalliances, what happened when you wanted to show you were more than just good friends?

Gary Cooper, the man whom Mae 'is that a gun in your pocket or are you just happy to see me?' West introduced to the silver screen, has obviously progressed to bigger things. In For Whom The Bell Tolls, *an inexpert Ingrid Bergman shows she's still got a lot to learn in the lip stakes.*

THE FIRST KISS

The first kiss is a real tester of a relationship. Like a geiger counter, the lip test will tell you whether to preserve a stiff upper lip or melt into a mouth-watering embrace. But your reaction to that kiss can bear little or no resemblance to how much you fancied someone before they kissed you. Just one kiss can turn you on or off.

Whether your kiss is powerful, erotic, shocking, tender, innocent, romantic, seductive, sweet, silly or enchanting, according to the old adage, it's all a matter of chemistry. Now, scientists seem to be proving the truth behind the folklore.

Rodin's famous marble treatment of sexual passion, The Kiss, *almost put his relationship with the American public on the rocks. The voice of the moral majority in America, vocal even back in the 1880s, decided the nude sculpture was too lewd for public view and banished it to a special room.*

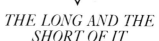

American skin expert Dr Bubba Nicholson blames our enthusiasm for kissing on something called semiochemicals.

Semiochemicals are substances which communicate a biological signal. Unlike pheronomes, which are discharged into the air, semiochemicals rest on the skin and are transmitted by touch. Nicholson believes that these semiochemicals are the product of the sebaceous glands which, at puberty, spring up inside the mouth and at the edges of the lips; they're also present in large quantities in small babies and pregnant women. According to Nicholson, 'the licking and sucking of these same interior surfaces during a passionate French kiss may effect the removal and transfer of sebum.'

During lovemaking, the heat of passion releases torrents of sebum, enhancing each partner's kissability. Thus, when a relationship is dying, kissing is the first activity to go. While other more obvious signs of sensuality may linger, the kiss seems to be the most delicate of human expressions – and totally dependent on the heart. A kiss shows a degree of love and sincerity that doesn't necessarily exist just by having sex.

THE LONG AND THE SHORT OF IT

According to the book *The Art of Kissing*, first published in the Twenties, 'It is . . . necessary that the man be taller than the woman. The psychological reason for this is that he must always give the impression of being his woman's superior, both mentally and especially physically. The physical reason . . . is that if he is taller than his woman, he is better able to kiss her. He must be able to sweep her into his strong arms and tower over her and look down into her eyes and cup her chin in his fingers and then bend over her face and plant his eager, virile lips on her moist, slightly parted, inviting ones. All this he must do with the vigour of an assertive male. And all these are impossible when the woman is the taller of the two . . . when the situation is reversed . . . the physical mastery is gone, the male prerogative is gone . . . nothing can be more disappointing.'

KISS AND TELL

The way you kiss is a giveaway about the way you love. Like a barometer, it can measure the state of your relationship. Expert marriage guidance

counsellors note that couples who hardly kiss at all may still be having sex. They've found that a lot of people find it easier to have sex with someone they no longer love than they do to kiss them. And if they do have sex, they tend to rush it, finding it difficult to kiss and touch their partner as they no longer feel good about them and in reality don't want to be close to them. The Marriage Guidance Council was so worried about this phenomenon that it published a booklet called *Kiss and Tell*. This booklet advises that if a couple put tenderness, warmth and passion into their kisses, they have nothing to worry about. But if they have got to the stage where all they give each other is a fleeting peck, it sounds as if love has gone.

LIP STYLE

Sexual kissing is quite distinct from social kissing – except in one instance: the goodnight kiss between new lovers. Depending on the experience of the couple involved, the social goodnight or farewell kiss has pretensions to inclusion in the sexual context. With luck and the emittance of the right amount of semiochemi-

RECORD SMOOCH-A-THON

The couple who hold the record for the longest kiss in a smooch-a-thon in Pennsylvania are Barbara Kane and Dino Delorean, who kissed non-stop for six days.

WATERY KISSES

The longest underwater kiss was 2 minutes 18 seconds by Toshiaki Shirai and Yukiko Nagata and took place on Channel 8 Fuji TV in Tokyo in April 1980.

THE LONGEST KISS

The longest kiss lasted 17 days and 9 hours and was practised in California by Patricia Hogan and Brad Spacy.

FUND RAISING KISSES

The largest number of people kissed was 4,106 at Newcastle University during a community action fund raising. They were kissed during an 8-hour period in March, 1983.

Ray Blazina and Bobbi Sherlock kissed for 130 hours, 2 mins and 17 seconds. Bobbi's boyfriend watched the charity marathon which was held in Pittsburgh, Pennsylvania.

cals, the goodnight kiss can easily turn into the first gesture of arousal, the first breakthrough into intimacy.

Once the goodnight kiss stage has been reached, the next moves follow very quickly. First, comes the single kiss when the lips are pressed gently together, which then becomes a vigorous moving pressure. Using the muscular action of the tongues, the partners work on each other's mouths as if drawing air from them. During deep kissing, both male and female penetrate each other's mouth with their tongues, exploring and licking the inside of each other's mouths. As passion heightens, the lips begin their quest for new territories to explore: the erogenous areas of the ear lobes, the toes, nipples, clitoris or penis. Along with the tips of the fingers, the clitoris and the tip of the penis, the tongue and lips are the

CAPITAL KISS

A 1982 survey showed that 59 percent of Londoners kiss on the lips each day, while only 38 percent of Scots do, and only 45 percent of people from Lancashire.

ARCH KISSING

Britain's long-running radio series, *The Archers*, introduced real lip kissing for the first time in 1979. Until then, kissing was simulated by coyly kissing the back of their own hands when the script called for a kiss.

most sensitive areas of the skin. Lip contact first begins when an infant takes milk either from its mother's breast or from a teat. Thus begins the association of comfort and love with lip contact.

During sexual arousal, mouths become swollen and red. Women's lips are usually slightly larger and fleshier than men's and many women exaggerate their size even further by wearing lipstick. As well as the difference between their lips, there is a great deal of difference in the way men and women kiss. A Canadian anthropologist, Pierre Maranda, discovered in one experiment that 97 percent of the women kept their eyes shut when kissing while only 37 percent of the men did. Perhaps women simply enjoy experiencing one sensual pleasure at a time while men like to savour two.

79

WHAT YOUR KISSING SAYS ABOUT YOU

There are all sorts of kisses – fickle, sweet, jaw-clenchers, earth shattering, erotic – but the way they're described is as revealing as the way they're practised. The way you kiss not only shows what kind of kisser you are, but also reveals a lot about your personality. How do you and your partner fare in the kiss-as-a-barometer stakes? Here's a list of right and wrong ways to kiss. If you can recognise the wrong ways, then your relationship may be on the rocks.

Right: a full-blooded kiss on the lips shows that you still desire each other and don't take each other for granted. You're likely to have a satisfying sex life and be able to talk things over. The good news for men is that surveys shows that men who kiss deeply are happier, healthier and more successful.

Right: kisses on your erogenous zones – ear lobes, tips of the fingers – means you care enough about each other to devote time to pleasing one another.

Wrong: a perfunctory peck on the cheek shows that you're growing apart and don't even want to be close to each other any more. Unless you start kissing and touching soon, you'll become ever more distant and out of touch.

Wrong: kisses plonked on the forehead show your partner still regards you as a wayward child and not a passionate, mature adult.

YOUR KISSES AND WHAT THEY REVEAL ABOUT YOUR PERSONALITY

Eyes closed

Kissing with your eyes closed means you're an incurable romantic, not that your partner is too ugly to contemplate! Closed eyes allow you to pursue your amorous fantasies – but therein lies the rub. You're such a romantic at heart that you fall in love as often as other couples quarrel. But then you do enjoy the flight, even if the landing is sometimes bumpy. Closed eyed kissers are also more likely to be women, who, according to surveys, are three times more likely than men to shut their eyes during kissing.

Michael Douglas (above), son of Kirk, tired of romancing the stone, has a shot at his new wife, Diandra, instead. But with all that hair obscuring his mouth, the best he could manage was a lipsided kiss.

London club owner Steve Strange's lip technique is enough to make his hair stand on end (right).

Eyes open

This is the other extreme. You're a down-to-earth realist who finds it difficult to fall in love – but when you do it's for keeps. Always on your guard, you find it hard to relax. When you kiss, you're probably also think-ing about your latest problem at work or whether to take the car to the garage for a service. You won't let yourself be carried away by the ecstasy of the moment. Still, if you're a man, chances are your partner won't notice anyway since she'll have her eyes closed!

Short, short, long

You're the overture to the symphony that follows – if anyone can wait that long. You don't like to commit your-self without a lot of thought. But once you've made up your mind you stick with your decision. Your symphony is definitely worth waiting for – the slow build-up hides a passionate and sen-sual nature.

Cuddler

You're prepared to spend some con-siderable time in foreplay because you're mature enough – or experi-enced enough – to know the pleasures of anticipation. While your lips seek our your partner's throat,

All she wanted was a close encounter – but he proved too much of an armful (left).

After his heroic sojourn in the Falklands, Prince Andrew (right) clearly hasn't yet learned how to relax. Still on the look-out for Exocets, he apparently views Lady Romsey's shoulder as a possible target.

The 'V-formation' kiss. Originated by RAF flying crew during the Second World War, who became used to doing everything in formation, it was said to be 'absolutely wizard' by its devotees. It is quite often followed by the 'victory roll'.

neck, cheek, your hands are busy caressing his or her body. Having learned the power that comes with understatement, your kisses aren't designed to be overwhelming. Your poise and self-confidence are reflected by your soft-spoken manner.

Clutcher

You're the sort of kisser who always holds on tightly to one part of your partner's body – perhaps your mother didn't pick you up enough and cuddle you as a child? At first, you appear to be a very dominant personality, so you attract weak people. But you're really very insecure – hence the clutching. You like to think you're running the relationship and can get out any time it suits *you*. But deep down, you're scared in case you're the one who gets dumped first. However, as long as you stick to partners who like a strong arm around them, you'll get along fine.

Public kisser

You don't get a thrill out of kissing unless you've got an audience. You crave the public recognition of your sexuality, if only to convince yourself. Quite likely, you were rather shy and backward in sexual matters as a teenager and are making up for it now – and letting everyone know about it. You're a let-down, though: once home, you're not as interested as you were in the street.

Getting dated: local Chelsea squaw makes the most of the last of the Mohicans.

Polo mint before kissers
Unless you've just eaten garlic snails, what are you really covering up? Perhaps you're not sure you actually like sex. Or maybe you're just very self-conscious, a teenager perhaps? Forget the mint and give in to passion.

Polo mint after kissers
You really don't like sex.

All-over kisser
You throw yourself into life wholeheartedly. Whether you're drinking, eating or making love, you devote all your attention to the task in hand. For you, life holds no restricted areas: on the football field, you roam from centre half to goalkeeper; in the office you're the boss who types her own letters. You view each sexual encounter as a completely new and exciting experience.

Lips closed
Closed lips means your mind is probably closed as well. You remember all momma's warnings about men who

Roy of the Rovers strays into the penalty area – it looks like he could be heading for another bookable offence. Still, you've got to hand it to him – he's always on the look-out for another scoring opportunity.

are only after one thing and you ensure they don't make it past the handshake. If you need physical release, you prefer to keep it to yourself. In life, as in love, you're a taker rather than a giver.

Puckered lips
The signal is on green, but you've never managed to make it past red. You're a pretender. You're offering a kiss that isn't really a kiss. You want everything your own way, whether it's kissing or in life. Puckered lips are very difficult to kiss back; they encourage the other person to back off. You pretend to play the game, but only by your own warped set of rules.

♡

BEAUTY AND THE BEAST

When people say the way he kisses is like an animal, they couldn't be more wrong. Some animals, such as the butterfly, don't kiss at all. The male house mouse licks the female's mouth. Sealions rub mouths and elephants sometimes put the tips of their trunks in one another's lips. Birds knock bills, cats squeeze noses, and pigeons practice cattaglottism.

How kissing can affect one's physical development: Ernest Borgnine demonstrates just how he shaped that famous nose with a kissing technique straight out of the pages of Greystoke.

Hard kisser

You're the original macho man. You haven't caught on to the fact that men are now allowed – even encouraged – to be tender and loving. You're still back in the days of hardbitten screen heroes like James Cagney. You don't have a lot of faith in yourself; you always want to make things happen, by force if necessary. Watch out – one day you may go too far. If a woman, you've probably been hurt by men in the past and are reluctant to show your tender side and expose your vulnerability.

French or soul kisser

You have no inhibitions about letting people know what you want. You're a very oral person: warm and passionate; a giver rather than a taker. You need intimacy with another person and sometimes leave yourself open to disappointment in your search for oneness. You're sensitive to other people's needs, too. Like your deep kisses, which ensure you taste all your lover's feelings, you suffer with friends, as well.

Hand kissers

You obviously majored in French. But be careful you don't overdose on that Gallic charm. You're keen to appear the perfect gent – opening doors, paying restaurant bills, helping your partner on with her coat – but there's a hungry predator underneath. Nine times out of ten, though, you strike lucky.

Slobbery kissers

Wet and mushy, saliva drools from the corners of your mouth, your partner's mouth and anywhere else around you. You have few inhibitions and if your lover makes your mouth water, so be it. You're not particularly concerned about your appearance; you might even go as far as to say that you actually enjoy the sloppiness that you've created. You may be good at kiss chase, but when it comes to making love, you're lousy.

The everyone kisser

You'll kiss anyone – parents, children, uncles, aunts, strangers, lovers, ex-lovers, the milkman. People often refer to you as a warm, giving person. Little do they realise that underneath that warm façade is someone who's terrified of physical contact. In fact you're just as likely to be passionate with the window cleaner as with your partner.

89

The non-kisser

If kissing is a way of non-verbal communication, then you're inarticulate. You indulge in sexual intercourse, but rarely kiss, showing that you want a relationship but not the emotional involvement. You're the sort of person who has experiences without ever experiencing anything. You're like a blackboard with no chalk.

The ear nibbler kisser

Are you nervous? Perhaps you've just given up smoking or are on a diet? Most probably, you're shy. Self-conscious about your looks, ear nibbling is a way of avoiding direct face to face confrontation. At business meetings, you let everyone have their say before taking the plunge. At parties, you appear to be the wallflower, but once you've had a chance to suss out the action, you're warm and friendly.

Love bite kissers

You're a human grafitti artist; you leave your mark wherever you go. Making love to someone isn't enough for you – everyone else has to know, too. As a teenager, with your first love, your probably carved both your initials on a tree. Most of your partners end up sporting polo necks, scarves, or thick, chunky necklaces.

Vacuum kissers

Not for the clean living, the vacuum kiss occurs when two people open their mouths and instead of caressing and exploring, suck inwards as though trying to draw the contents out of an egg. Soon, the air is drawn tightly out of both mouths and they adhere together so tightly that there is pain instead of pleasure. When you've had enough, don't try to tear your mouth away or you'll end up summoning the bomb squad with the noise you make. First, simply open a corner of your mouth so that some of the air can escape.

The vacuum kiss is an aggressive type of kiss, revealing someone who likes to rush their partner into love-making rather than let them decide for themselves.

The nibbler

More like an aperitif, it's hoped that this is followed by the main course. A nibble can easily turn into a bite, however, so maybe you're too inhibited to reveal your inner desires completely and are covering up your aggression.

DJ Dave Lee Travis finds he has bitten off more than he can chew when he encounters former beekeeper Mari Wilson, who forbears from telling him to buzz off.

STAR KISSES

AQUARIUS

20 Jan – 19 Feb

As an Aquarian, Ronald Reagan's instincts are humanitarian; in his personal life he favours co-operation, following a policy of entente cordiale with wife Nancy and close friends while maintaining a cool front with the East. A typical Aquarian, he can't bear bust-ups in relationships – whether personal or political – an idyllically happy married life has given him little experience in the art of breaking up and making up. When smiling, his mouth shows that he's willing to be flexible; rigid, it says much about his own rigidity once he's made up his mind.

PISCES

20 Feb – 20 Mar

Marlon Brando, the sultry star with the sulky looks won fame and Oscars for his roles in *On The Waterfront* and *The Godfather*. But it was his part in *Last Tango in Paris*, co-starring with Maria Schneider and a half pound of butter, which brought him notoriety. Idealistic and dreamy, as are many Pisceans, he thought he had discovered his Utopia when, during the filming of *Mutiny on the Bounty* in 1962, he fell in love with a beautiful Tahitian girl and adopted her lifestyle. Despite his increasing bulk, he still retains those generously-proportioned, beautifully shaped lips which betray a personality addicted to satisfaction of the senses.

ARIES

21 Mar – 20 Apr

Charlie Chaplin had a fund of ceaseless energy – starring, directing and producing films as well as marrying and fathering children often enough to earn himself a reputation in Hollywood and the press as a womanizer. As an Arian, his leadership qualities and courage are revealed by his decision to set up his own film production company. But the less aggressive and more emotional side of his nature can be seen from his rather 'feminine' mouth:

curved and full and signifying his passion.

TAURUS

21 Apr – 20 May

A typical Taurean, with his sensual nature, Valentino portrayed all the dark, brooding mystery of the Latin temperament. Although his mouth was small, his lips were generous and full and his uninhibited kisses aroused illicit dreams in thousands of female breasts. A conservative nature, at odds with his rampant screen sensuality was revealed by the smallness of his mouth and this quality came out in his private life where off-screen lovers never quite achieved the romance and fulfilment of those on screen.

GEMINI

21 May – 20 Jun

Luckily for Errol Flynn, he was born under the sign of Gemini, traditionally great advocates and persuasive talkers, especially as he had to defend himself in court more than once on charges related to his romantic adventures with very young ladies. Unfortunately, like a typical Gemini, he couldn't concentrate on anything for any length of time, preferring to escape into his own world through the whisky bottle. His thin lips belie his much-publicised sexuality, which is hinted at in the curve of his upper lip.

CANCER

21 Jun – 20 Jul

Sylvester Stallone, the all-American, muscle-bound, invincible hero who Rockyeted to stardom with a fighting formula, belies the kind and caring, protective qualities inherent in most Cancerians. Having fought for the title in *Rocky*, Syllie Stallone has made sure of the title rôle ever since. As his body has rid itself of all soft tissue, so has his mind until Stallone the actor has become the ultimate fighting machine. His screen characters, both in the *Rocky* and the *Rambo* series, are in line with his jutting jaw and well-developed, protruding lips which betray a pugnacious personality, quick to react.

93

LEO

21 Jul – 21 Aug

It's singularly appropriate that Richard Gere, the man who is known as 'the king of the kissers' for his steamy roles in *American Gigolo* and *An Officer And A Gentleman*, should be born under the sign of Leo, that fiery king of the jungle. His technique is to close his eyes (revealing his romantic nature), open his mouth and munch. A little lacking in subtlety perhaps? But his lipnotic power over women seems to have waned recently as he struggles to prove that behind his sexy image lies an actor of great talent and a man of sensitivity.

VIRGO

22 Aug – 22 Sept

Star of the odd film or two but arguably more famous for her romantic liaisons, Britt Ekland displays few of the signs of a true Virgoan. Perhaps she'd been so busy trying to be a *True Britt* that her astrological characteristics had been dimmed, but 'hardworking' and 'prudish' would probably not be the first two words to trip off one's tongue if asked briefly to describe this Swedish actress. Reformed by her marriage to Slim Jim, at one point references to her being 'all mouth' indicated more about her habit of revealing all about her past lovers than the fact that this orifice is of generous proportions.

LIBRA

23 Sept – 22 Oct

Margaret Thatcher, born under the sign of Libra, would doubtless be pleased to know that in a study carried out in the Seventies, there proved to be more Librans among politicians than any other star sign. As a young woman, Mrs Thatcher's lips had a much softer line; now, they're thinner with only a very slightly defined Cupid's bow betraying any softness in her nature. The wide mouth and fuller lower lip reveal that although she's an obstinate character who's prepared to argue her case through to the bitter end, she is very loyal to friends and allies, often refusing to drop colleagues who have become liabilities despite the risk to her own reputation.

SCORPIO

23 Oct – 22 Nov

A man who, for most of his working life, was referred to by three digits, Sean Connery's star sign Scorpio fitted him admirably for his role as the penetrating but secretive and ruthless secret service agent, James Bond. Having spent some of his youth as a coffin polisher, his screen success reversed his fortunes and he made a healthy living out of polishing off opponents for the coffin makers. Although guilty of giving a lot of lip to his bosses back in Whitehall, his narrow upper lip reveals a careful self-control.

SAGITTARIUS

23 Nov – 20 Dec

Bo Derek gets ten out of ten for enthusiasm, a quality she owes to her star sign, Sagittarius. Only enthusiasm could have carried her through the waves of criticism following her attempts to capitalise on her success in the film *10*. Despite her 'no improvement shown, could do a lot better' report from *Bolero*, Miss Derek certainly deserves high marks for oral interplay. One thing's for sure: husband, mentor and film producer John Derek won't let this adverse reaction put him off asking backers to put their money where her mouth is.

CAPRICORN

21 Dec – 19 Jan

Capricorns are usually aspirational. Climbing steadily up the career ladder, was Marlene Dietrich who transformed herself Cinderella-like from a rather frumpy German fraulein to one of the most svelte and sexy stars Hollywood had ever seen. A wide mouth showed her inherently generous nature but her narrow lips revealed she had her feet firmly on the ground. In private, she remained faithful to the man she had met and married before stardom, although in later life they actually lead fairly separate lives.

95

POLITICAL KISSING

Once upon a time, the quantity of a politician's votes was roughly equivalent to the number of children he had kissed during the run-up to an election. Garnering votes by displaying osculatory affection for infants was a way of political life. Canvassing candidates swooped on unsuspecting babes-in-arms and smooched with the little mites for the benefit of the ever-present camera.

Then, mothers wised up to the health problems associated with such overtly affectionate behaviour, while TV cameras discovered that all this interest in babies was obscuring the fact that far more salacious embraces were taking place out of the camera's view. By the mid-Sixties, the public had had their fill of MPs' private lives and the art of political onelipmanship died.

—— KISSING AT NUMBER 10 ——

A younger generation of hardbitten MPs surfaced, who believed that the only place to give lip was in the House. And with a woman Prime Minister installed at number 10, the kiss received a definite political embargo.

During her climb to the top, though, a well-turned cheek had not always gone amiss with Mrs Thatcher. In her early electioneering days, the woman who took away children's school milk had a lot of pram swooping to do to soften her image. In her bid for the leadership, her eloquence smothered the tongue-tied, hand-shaking incumbent. Warm and melting in victory, she embraced top

Whoever said Mrs Thatcher lacked sincerity? As we all know, she just has trouble with her eyesight. Here, she misses yon youngster and plants a true blue smacker straight on the photographer's zoom lens.

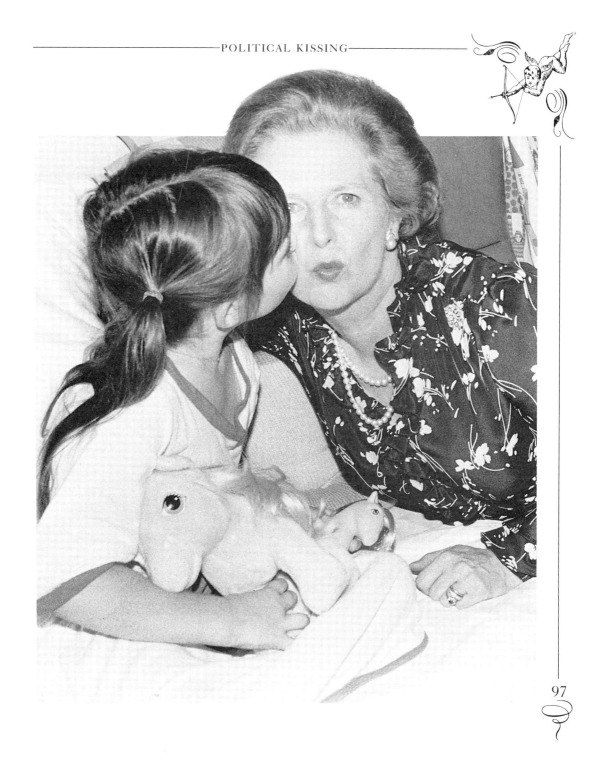

party acolytes such as defeated rival, Willie Whitelaw.

But her time in office has ironed out the soft edges. Even personal favourites such as Norman Tebbit, who are high up in the political pecking order, wouldn't dare to kiss her for fear of being thought chauvinist and condescending.

— KISSING IN THE HOUSE —

Nowadays in the House, MPs are all hands – and they're not just taking the lead from their leader. Male MPs can no longer afford to be seen giving a friendly peck to their secretaries for fear of starting another Parkinson scandal, while female MPs don't want to be labelled 'the little woman'. Even husband and wife teams keep their kissing for the home, not the House. Peter and Virginia Bottomley, both Conservative MPs, find the thought of displaying their affection openly in front of their colleagues vulgar. In the early hours of the morning, however, after an all-night sitting, it's not unknown for exhausted MPs – male and female – to share a comradely hug.

Of course, each party has its own unofficial kissing manifesto. The

Being an incurable romantic – in the best Welsh tradition – Neil Kinnock (top) prefers to keep his eyes closed when kissing. But Glenys got the Claus out after this oral constitutional with strippogram Mother Christmas.

Lord Wilson (far left) demonstrating his mastery of 'the foot in the door and mouth' technique.

It's supposed to be lucky to be kissed by a chimney sweep on your wedding day. In this case, Joy Crispin (below) had to be happy with a peck on the cheek from new father-in-law Harold Wilson, after marrying his son John in 1968.

99

Labour Party, in an effort to show solidarity with the East, are keen huggers. Comrade A takes one step forward and grasps comrade B's left arm (in Russia, this is to make sure comrade B doesn't fall over; in Britain, it's usually because the two embracers have diametrically opposed views, despite belonging to the same party), with his right hand. Bringing his other foot forward to meet the first, comrade A then moves close to B, pulls him towards him and, with his left arm, hugs his back. Another variation practised by comrades in grief or those whose friendship goes back through several political pogroms, is to pat the back three or four times before retreating. Recently, top Labour ministers have been flying to the East to take lessons.

Mouths are not such a pressing problem for the Liberal/SDP Alliance. Preferring the informal approach, David Owen and David Steel think nothing of greeting Shirley Williams with a salutary kiss.

A graphic illustration of 'the sexuality of power': here we see the most potent combination in the Western Alliance. While US President Ronald Reagan makes a play for the Prime Ministerial lobes, Mrs Thatcher employs that slender left hand to give him the elbow.

FOREIGN HABITS

Ministers who've served their time in the EEC have definitely taken to the Continental habit. Eurocrats in Belgium have been reported as adopting the practice of greeting women friends with kisses on both cheeks. Whether they will import the habit into this country when their time is up, is another matter. While at home the kiss is in recession, on the international front, it has never been more in evidence. In the game of onelipmanship, the American First couple have led the rest of the world. A plain old romantic at heart, Ronald insists on sealing their love with a kiss whenever the opportunity arises. Unlike the Russians, Ronald and Nancy's kisses attest to their active lifestyle as well as showing the human side of the world's top pair. And Ronald learned his art in a good school: Hollywood.

Unfortunately, like most fanatics, Ronald feels obliged to convert the rest of the political world to his way of kissing. On a visit to the States, Mrs Thatcher was subjected to the B film version of the kiss (he keeps the A film version specially for his wife). Her stiff back showed what she

101

thought of this unwarranted intrusion. Moreover, the kiss caused a few stiff backs back in Britain, too. Political commentators, quick to take umbrage at any penetration of the Iron Lady's armour, didn't take kindly to Reagan's intended compliment, feeling he'd treated her as a co-star rather than as his leading lady. Reagan wasn't the first US politician to upset political protocol. When Walter Mondale visited Israel in 1978, he greeted its leader, the late Golda Meir, with a peck on the cheek. Her countrymen were astonished at his audacity.

But while Ronald and Nancy may engage in endless smoochathons, it's a different story for their political rivals. For vice-presidential candidate, Geraldine Ferraro, the run-up to the last election really was touch and go. While Reagan gave top billing to his own public amour propre, his aides made sure there was no hanky panky in the opposite camp. Where two male contenders would have been expected to hug, pat each other on the back, put their arms around each other's shoulders, raise their locked hands together in the air, Presidential candidate Walter Mondale had to keep his distance from his female running mate. The two unfortunate politicians were caught between two stools: on the one hand, over-demonstrative touching and kissing might be seen as evidence of a male chauvinist attitude – or worse, an affair; on the other, the naturally demonstrative American people might find the pair's standoffishness chilly and unsympathetic. Moreover, politicians in the US are more demonstrative than their counterparts anywhere else in the world. So while Ferraro was hugged, kissed, and embraced from New York to Ohio, Mondale didn't so much as get a peck in.

Unlike America, in France political kissing is as common as social kissing – whether the person in question is male or female. There, there's no outcry from a repressed media, no insinuations of 'les grandes affaires'. But the French political kiss has undergone one hundred percent inflation recently: politicians – male to male, male to female, female to female – now give each other two kisses on the cheek both on greeting and on bidding au revoir.

Italians, despite their mucho macho image, would never dare to bring sex into the political arena.

In addition to his arsenal of MX missiles, US President Ronald Reagan has undiminished reserves of lip power to call on – even in his seventies. Here we see him (left) preparing his First Lady for take-off just prior to her departure for the Royal Wedding in 1981.

After the last election campaign debacle, Walter Mondale receives a consoling embrace from his domestic running mate.

103

The Eastern Blockbuster – Erich Honeker, after a couple of cheeky flank attacks, meets the Russian offensive head on with this classic Napoleonic move on the centre.

They might pinch a girl's derrière, but they would never hug or kiss a female colleague. As one leading Roman parliamentarian put it, 'It would violate the rules of manly and political dignity and would only cause horror and scandal.'

When looking for the country with the most dignified political greeting, you've got to hand it to the West Germans. Anxious not to invade a visiting politician's *lebensraum*, they eschew the peck on the cheek in favour of the chivalrous, but long-forgotten art, of hand kissing. The politicians are copying an action which is now all the rage in West Germany. Thirty years ago, only one

East German leader Ulbricht takes his hat off to former Russian premier Leonid Brezhnev before retreating to the Kremlin to discuss life behind the wall.

third of Germans approved of hand kissing, the rest viewing it as vaguely decadent. Now, the number who find hand kissing 'nice and romantic' has shot up to 50 percent. Hand kissing originally came from Austria where it was practised with a certain fitnesse. The man bent down and raised the woman's hands to his lips, but there was no physical contact.

Some politicians have been known to get carried away by the ardour of their kisses, leading to embarrassing breaches of behaviour. The late Israeli Prime Minister, Golda Meir, was said to have spent days dodging Menachem Begin in the Israeli Parliament's dining-room because he insisted on kissing her hand every time they met.

Unlike the rest of the world, where kisses are less intimate at home and more affectionate abroad, in Russia the reverse is the case. Top Russians, who've fought together – perhaps even fought each other – to get to their elevated positions, frequently kiss each other on the lips, reserving the less intimate bear hug for visiting dignitaries. But if a Russian leader kisses and hugs another, the other may kiss and hug him back only if he is of equal status.

Hugging seems to be particularly popular on the occasion of Russian state funerals and marches past. Elderly statesmen, anxious to ward off the cold, are usually so ancient that they can't even hit the mark any more, ending up more often than not with their kisses landing somewhere between the ear and the back of the head. But on the whole the Russians are not a very close race, if only because they wear so many layers of clothes.

INTERNATIONAL KISSING

ip to lip, lip to cheek, nose to nose, mouth to foot . . . every country has its own particular kissing style.

But in some countries, natives curl up their lips at the thought of mouth to mouth contact. Some tribes get their sexual thrills from pressing noses or faces, while others practise mouth to mouth and nose to nose contact simultaneously. In others still, kissing takes the form of placing the lips close to the partner's face and inhaling.

Movie-makers must take some of the blame for spreading the habit of kissing to places where no man's lips had ever gone before. In Japan in the Twenties, for instance, kissing was reserved solely for children and the censors were still cutting screen embraces out of all the American films they imported. Meanwhile, in remote parts of China, children were warned by their mothers to beware of the 'white man's kiss' as it was thought to be suggestive of cannabalism.

In the Western world, lip kissing goes back a long way – its origins have been traced back as far as the ancient Romans. The Greeks don't seem to have been practised in the art – they didn't even have a word for it.

In the pioneering days of the United States, kissers weren't quite as demonstrative as they are today. In the Eastern States and Canada, covered bridges or kissing bridges were among the most popular places for a little quiet courting. At one time, there were at least one thousand in the province of Quebec alone and a like number in New Brunswick, but fire, decay and spring floods reduced their numbers drastically.

Today, social kissing is very popular in America and there are very few

Ever been kissed by someone whose name completely escapes you? Barbara Stanwyck searches her palm for clues to Linda (Dynasty) Evans's identity.

107

(Top left) Sylvester Stallone and Valerie Perrine
(Bottom left) Taylor and Gonzalez (Top right) Joan
Collins and John James (Bottom right) John
Forsythe, *in a soppy soap* Love Boat in China.

Clint Eastwood (Top) receives a congratulatory hug from fellow Hollywood star Charlton Heston.

Burton and Taylor (Bottom) with that five-star look of utter bliss.

rules. In true democratic fashion, Americans have even discarded the natural pecking order attached to the kiss. In trend-setting New York, it is now acceptable for rich women to exchange pecks on the cheek with the head waiter as they enter and leave the better restaurants.

SOAP AND THE KISS

Americans didn't have to cross the Atlantic to learn the art of social kissing. Their role models – the Carringtons, Colbys and Ewings – were right in their own living-rooms. They switched on to soap and got turned on to the kiss as a social weapon. Even TV role models, though, can be given marks out of ten for expertise. America, the country of lists – best dressed, worst dressed, sexiest bottom, widest smile, largest bank balance, thickest social diary – has now brought out a good kissing guide. Like the *Good Food Guide* in Britain, the *Good Kiss Guide* gives star ratings, from one to five, to screen smoochers. Masters and mistresses of the Hollywood art include Liz Taylor and Jacqueline Bisset. The *Guide* is particularly impressed with Ms Taylor's mouthful of contributions, giving her a five-star rating every time she puckers up because of the 'look of utter bliss on her face'. Jacqueline Bisset, meanwhile, was recommended for her cool looks which hid 'an inborn fire', while Cary Grant is reported to be 'suave . . . kisses with charm and humour'. Burt Reynolds gets a top rating alongside Ms Taylor for kisses that exude 'pure, raw sex'.

The *Guide* gives a thumbs down, however, to some of our most popular screen heroes and heroines. Bottom of the list is fallen angel Farrah Fawcett, who joins her male co-stars in the guide, Clint Eastwood, Sylvester Stallone and Charles Bronson. Eastwood is accused of wanting to get it over with quickly, while Stallone is reputed to be very physical but sloppy and Bronson is rebuked for not having enough tenderness.

Of course, soaps have travelled the world, converting the non-kissers as they went. From Lapland to Mongolia, TV viewers whose own method of expressing sexual passion was to press nose to cheek, breathe in deeply, lower their eyelids and smack their lips, were astounded at the Western habit of lip pressing. To the Swahili tribe, accustomed

PAPAL EMBRACE

In Brazil there's a man called José Moura whose life's ambition is to kiss every visiting dignitary. His most famous embraces to date are the Pope and Frank Sinatra.

to getting turned on by smelling the opposite sex's genitalia, lip kissing must have seemed tame in comparison.

But despite the efforts of the Lorimar Production Company, eskimos still ping noses, Papuans and some Indian hill tribes still rub noses while Trobrian Islanders have the waspish habit of biting each other's eyelashes. In fact, Papuans place a lot of emphasis on nose rubbing. In the Mount Hagen district, when girls are of marriageable age, a nose rubbing or courting ceremony is held so that the young men can choose a bride. During the ceremony, the men move round the circle to each of the girls in turn, even though they may already have a particular girl in mind.

In the Mount Hagen district of New Guinea, a man chooses his bride only after a courting ritual involving a nose-rubbing ceremony. Eligible girls sit in a circle while the men sniff out a future mate.

— LA MÉTHODE FRANÇAISE —

Naturally, it's the French who have the honour of having a kiss named after them. To tongue-tied teenagers in Britain, French kissing brings the thrill of the first 'proper' kiss. In France, to close friends – man-to-man, man-to-woman and woman-to-woman – the two kisses, one on each cheek, are simply a social greeting. Friends who've known each other for years and years may give each other three kisses – left, right and then left again. Within families, the French practise a time-consuming four kisses, two on one cheek and two on the other. French family gatherings tend to be long, drawn-out affairs.

Hand kissing is also very popular in France, particularly among descendants of the ancient regime. Like the French courtiers of old, the man does not let his lips touch the hand, but hovers a few centimetres above it like a butterfly. Like most aristocrats, he knows, too, that protocol decrees that only the hand of a married woman may be kissed.

French kisses, though, are only part of the French way of greeting. Whereas in Britain, a salute is followed immediately by general conversation, in France, the salutation centres on the last time you met, what you said and did, what the changes have been since that time and the health of your family – from children to grandparents. Only when this ritual has been completed, can you get on with the conversation.

—— THE INTERNATIONAL —— COLLECTION

West Germans, ever keen to do the correct thing, have eschewed lip or cheek kissing in favour of hand kissing. They take the lady's hand, bend down and bring their mouth close without actually making contact. Imported from Austria, hand kissing is widespread among professional Germans and those with social pretensions. However, it's rare among the lower middle class and totally unknown to blue collar workers.

In India, kissing is still considered a very private act, so much so that it's only recently that kisses have been

Known as the kiss with the local bicycle. This kiss transcends all national barriers and for men in many countries, is likely to be the first full-blown kiss they ever experience. Later on they develop more discerning taste and leave bicycles behind for more sophisticated venues such as the back of a Renault 5.

♡ REVOLTING KISS

When French revolutionary Danton heard that his wife had died in his absence, he rushed back to Paris, went straight to the cemetery and ordered the gravediggers to disinter the body. Then he bellowed phrases of adoration and kissed her decaying flesh.

permitted on screen. Recently, an Indian film actress who kissed Prince Charles on the cheek (left) when he was in Bombay, was accused of 'projecting a false image of Indian womanhood abroad' and ordered to appear in court.

After Americans, Australians are probably the most uninhibited kissers in the world, throwing themselves into the activity with gusto.

Russians are another race who are generous with their kisses, greeting compatriots with a triple giant bear hug. Oddly for a country with no class system, the pecking order is rigid: you may only hug a comrade back if you are of equal station; if unequal, you simply submit to his embrace with dignity. At Christmas and Easter, this system is dropped and kisses are distributed indis-

criminately. At state funerals, widows of top leaders are not prevented from planting a last kiss on their husband's lips before the burial ceremony. In South America, too, kissing the dead is becoming widespread. In some states, where soap opera screenwriters have reached god-like status, six-mile long queues form in a bid to give the departed writer an osculatory farewell.

In Abu Dhabi, even social kissing gets the thumbs down. Draconian laws exist to punish those who transgress the rigid social code. In 1983, an unmarried Asian couple were jailed for kissing on the cheeks while alone together in a room.

Sexually attractive Polynesians are very easy to spot: they have little or no eyebrows. The Polynesian kiss, known as a mitakuku, is a very aggressive affair; it involves tearing off hairs from a loved one's eyebrows with one's teeth.

The Chinese are turned on by tickling the soles of one another's feet; the Persians fold their hands and bow; the Swiss kiss with a single cheek to cheek embrace, while a Hindu Kush tribe kiss three times on the cheek and then once each on both hands.

IS KISSING GOOD FOR YOU?

edically, the news about kissing is good . . . and bad. Mouths have come under the microscope recently and turned up all sorts of hidden facts. The bad news is that kissing can cause epidemics, sore throats, swollen glands, and can strain the heart – both medically and emotionally. Every time you kiss, your heart beats much faster causing your life span to be reduced by three minutes, according to some American doctors. On the lighter side, each kiss uses up 3 calories; 1,000 a week means you'll be 1 lb lighter, but you'll also have 50 hours deducted from your life!

The kiss of death scientists have also come up with other passion killers. During mouth to mouth contact, the researchers say, kissers can exchange up to 250 bacteria as well as a handful of viruses and parasites. They've also discovered that kissing has the same effect as stress: thyroid activity shoots up, glucose production rises and the body's production of insulin stops. Diabetics should always carry around a lump of sugar to sweeten their lover's kiss.

It seems that too much kissing can harm your health. Athletes in particular are at risk from the kissing bug, officially known as Infectious Mononucleosis. A glandular fever caused by a virus believed to be passed on in saliva, the only remedy is plenty of rest and quiet. Over-passionate kissing can result in a very nasty syndrome called temporomandibular joint disfunction – or sore jaws!

When lovers talk about kissing being a drug, they don't realise how true that is. A kiss can be more effective than morphine in helping to reduce pain as it's ten times more powerful than that drug. And when a

Blondie (Debbie Harry), obviously perplexed as to why Chris Steen wears his glasses while kissing, yet still keeps his eyes closed.

117

This wallflower hibernates while her friend goes in for a bit of cross pollination.

mother tells her injured child she'll 'kiss it better', that's exactly what she does. A mother's kiss activates the production of natural, pain-killing hormones in the body, known as endorphins.

Kissing is responsible for the bonding feeling mothers have for their new-born babies. According to dermatologists, sebaceous glands along the borders of the lips, produce a sexy chemical during the last three months of pregnancy and after the baby is born. New-born babies respond by producing the same chemicals around their lips. These semiochemicals are exchanged during kissing to induce bonding or love. It takes a year for the kissing chemicals to decline to their normal level. But while it is around, there is a much greater urge to kiss.

DUMMY KISS

5 members of the St. John's Clifton Combined Division, York, maintained a kiss of life for 240 hours with 224,029 inflations between 26 July and 5 August 1981. Fortunately the patient was a dummy.

Blondes have more fun . . . but in this case, Mr Stewart made a rod for his own back when he dumped wife Alana and resumed his wenching ways. Alana fought like a tiger for more of the cash.

Kissers who like to nibble or bite will be pleased to know that dentists give kissing the thumbs up. They have discovered that kissing encourages saliva, which washes off food and lowers the level of acid in the mouth. Described as nature's way of giving your teeth a shower, kissing is probably one of the best ways to produce saliva in the mouth. The saliva acts as a rinsing agent and research shows that rinsing the mouth is a fine way of combating tooth decay. It prevents a build-up of plaque, which is what causes decay. Kissing also involves a trade-off in enzymes, which play the same role as antibiotics.

119

BEAUTIFUL LIPS

raditionally, hot lips have always been full and generous, wide and pouting. Yet not everyone is as well-endowed as the Mick Jaggers of this world ... which is where clever make-up comes in. Make sure your mouth looks kissable, and he'll never feel the difference.

Does your mouth suit your face?

1 If you've got large eyes, your mouth should be full and generous.

2 If your face is large, make your mouth large; if your face is round, avoid full lips or you'll look even rounder.

3 If your nose dominates your face, make your mouth larger so that attention is focused on your mouth, not your nose.

4 A large mouth overpowers a small, delicate face. Follow the tips for thinner lips and a smaller mouth.

—— *STEP-BY-STEP GUIDE* ——
TO THE PERFECT MOUTH

1 Cover the edges of your mouth with foundation and/or powder so that any mistakes can be rectified.

2 Use a well-sharpened lip pencil in a colour which tones in with your chosen lip colour to define the outline of your lips. First, define your cupid's bow, then work on upper and lower lips, defining inwards from the corners.

3 Fill in lip colour by painting gently with a lip brush. Do not overload brush with colour, but feather on until you've achieved required depth.

4 Brighter lip colours should be used for darker skins; yellow teeth look whiter with bright lipstick in wine or pink shades.

5 Outlining lips with a lip pencil rather than a brush keeps the colour confined to the lips. This is important for women with wrinkles running

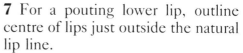

from the lips, a minor problem.

6 Upper and lower lips should be balanced in size. If top lip is thinner, paint just outside the natural lip line and just inside the line of the lower lip. If the lower lip is thinner, reverse the procedure.

7 For a pouting lower lip, outline centre of lips just outside the natural lip line.

8 Add lip gloss in the centre of the lips only – never at the sides. Lip gloss protects the colour and adds shine.

PROBLEM MOUTHS

Thin lips

Thin lips look fuller by drawing a pale pencil outline just outside the natural line of the lips and then painting in a slightly fuller lip line in a shade darker than your lipstick. Fill in with a deeper tone, blending the two shades together. Add a dab of lip gloss on the centre of both lips for fullness. Another method is to use two shades of lip colour, light over dark.

Thin upper lip

To enlarge a thin upper lip, outline lip line with pencil, making it wider across the bow and narrowing it down as you draw out to artificial corners. Use a light shade of lipstick and plenty of lip gloss. Pucker up as if you are about to blow a kiss and apply lip gloss, confining it to a very small area in the centre of the lips.

Thin lower lip

Extend the line of the lower lip very carefully beyond its natural boundaries. Fill in the lower lip with a colour that is several shades lighter than the upper lip, but in the same shade family. This will equalise a thin lower lip with that of the upper.

Full lips

If your mouth is the first thing people notice or you were known as 'rubber lips' at school, it's time you underplayed your lips and let your personality do a little of the talking. Outline lips with a lighter-coloured lip pencil, staying within your natural lip line. Then fill in with a darker colour. Very pale and very bright colours should be avoided, as should lip gloss.

One lip fuller than the other

Balance both lips by outlining with a pencil first and then using a darker colour on the full lip than on the thin one. Lip gloss can also be added to the less full lip to equalise fullness.

Small mouth

Conversely, a small mouth can appear wider if the pencil outline is extended just beyond the natural corners and then filled in with colour.

Wide mouth

Wide mouths can look smaller if pencil outlines stop just short of the corners and lip colour is faded out at the sides with lip gloss applied in the middle of the mouth only.

Wrinkled mouth

Defining lips with a lip pencil helps to prevent the lip colour running into the wrinkles beyond the lips. A base of foundation and powder also helps to disguise fine wrinkles. Avoid pale shades – or you'll look washed out. Dark tones can look ageing.

For a Cupid's bow use a densely covering foundation to blur the natural outline of the lips and apply colour with a lip brush very precisely.

HOT TIPS

Kissing has its dark side, too. In a giant leap into depravity, witches use the innocent pleasures of kissing and sex in their own licentious ceremonies. In macabre rituals celebrating the occult, the five-fold kiss plays an integral part.

Newcomers to the circle of white witches undergo an initiation ceremonial in which kissing is the final seal signifying membership of the coven. Aspiring white witches first take off all their clothes. Coven leaders believe that when you are naked, it is more difficult to lie. Then they are blindfolded – removal of which would take away the veil of ignorance – and a sword is pointed at their breasts. The sword is symbolic of their fate should they bring witchcraft into disrepute or surrender up their brothers and sisters in the craft.

Every part of the body is then measured and each measurement written down; the sum total is the number of days that the initiate will live.

Just before the new witch enters the magic circle, with her hands and feet firmly tied, she is asked, 'How do you come here? In peace, or love or wisdom?' She is then led round the

Better the devil you know . . . witches who find themselves falling behind are encouraged by their fellow coven members to kiss and make up.

circle while each member of the coven whispers words of advice in her ear. Then comes the high point of the ceremonial when the coven leader kisses her five times – on each foot, each knee and on the solar plexus. The five-fold kiss marks her initiation into the coven as a fully-fledged white witch.

History provides another macabre instance of the dark side of kissing. When Sir Walter Raleigh was executed on the orders of King James I in 1617, his widow – a former maid of honour to Queen Elizabeth I, whom he had secretly married – carried his preserved head around in a red velvet bag. A high-ranking cleric of the time, Bishop Goodman, admitted that he had been called upon to kiss the cold lips many times and had done so in an attempt to please the grieving widow. Until her death at the age of 82, she persisted in encouraging visitors to gaze upon her dead husband's face.

LITERARY KISSES

The kiss has been a vital part of literature from Shakespeare and John Donne to Barbara Cartland. But it was only with the popularity of the 'bruised lips' variety of novel, when a whole generation of readers thrilled to the bodice-ripping embraces of

The Mills & Boon spoon defined as (Oxford Shorter Snogging Dictionary 1984 Vol V1): 'Passionate and violent osculation normally accompanied or preceded by doomed love, forbidden lust or tragic accident. Parties involved must include delicate fragile, fair-skinned female and swarthy, square-jawed muscular foreign polo player. Non-garlic eater preferred.'

125

hunky heroes, that the kiss became the pivotal centre of the story.

Purveyors of these paperback romances know the value of a kissing formula. And their formula has been proved to work – in 1979, Harlequin (whose more familiar offspring is Mills & Boon) sold 168 million copies worldwide. Mills & Boon have been

A precariously balanced Romeo assaults Juliet's balcony in the best tradition of the SAS before necking with the young Miss Capulet.

joined in this flood of romance by Silhouette, Sapphire Romances, Nightshades, Circle of Love, Sweet Dreams and Candlelight Ecstasy, among others.

Nothing is left to chance when it comes to throbbing passion between the pages of these well-thumbed novelettes. Everything, down to the last blissful sigh, is planned and calculated for maximum effect. Many publishing houses even issue passion style sheets for their authors' guidance. In 1980 Silhouette Books' *A–Z to Success* ran as follows: 'Love Scenes: descriptions of love-making should be sensuous with some details. They cannot be limited to "he kissed her passionately" ... nudity is permissible but it should not be too graphic. The only pain permitted is the sweet pain of fulfilled (or unfulfilled) desire.'

SCHOOL FOR KISSING

Kissing on the stage is as carefully choreographed as that between the covers of any Mills & Boon romance. Drama schools, realising that there's an art to show-stealing kissing, are now offering kissing lessons to budding actors and actresses. At Bretton

Hall College in Yorkshire, the head of drama says, 'There is an art to kissing. It can mean so many different things. The kiss can be anything from just a friendly greeting to a strong sexual signal and anyone who wants to be successful on stage must know how to do them all properly.' Students at Bretton Hall's kissing workshops trace the development of the kiss from the Elizabethan period through ritual kissing as practised in religion, to kissing as a greeting and eventually to sexual and passionate kissing.

KISSING CUSTOMS

Good luck: Being kissed by a chimney sweep on your wedding day – whether you're a bride or a groom – is a sign of good luck and a long and happy marriage.

Bad luck: In Yorkshire, if a young man is caught kissing his sweetheart indoors, it's bad luck. However, the canny Yorkshireman can reverse the luck by immediately throwing kiss-money on the table. If he doesn't, then his sweetheart's sisters or friends burn a hole in his coat or cut off his buttons.

KISSING GATE

England had its own version of the kissing bridges frequented by early American and Canadian lovers; only here, it was called the Kissing Gate. The kissing gate was the haunt of courting couples like the back seat of a car in the Sixties. Kissing gates allow one person to work the gate around themselves. Two people trying to do so get very close . . . hence the name.

Kissing gates, which both parties pass through together in close proximity, were a hazard of the countryside for ladies unaccustomed to the courting customs of country gents.

127

ACKNOWLEDGEMENTS

To David Heslam for his encouragement and support; Philip Jenkinson for his invaluable and generous help; to Robert Smith for his insight and faith; to Joan Tinney for her professional guidance and to Geoffrey Austen for his help with research.

DESIGNER: Roger Daniels

PICTURE CREDITS

KOBAL COLLECTION: pages 7, 9, 13, 14, 17, 21, 22, 25, 26, 28, 31, 32, 34, 35, 37, 39, 40, 42, 44, 46, 47, 49, 50, 52, 75.

RONALD GRANT ARCHIVE: pages 18, 54.

SYNDICATION INTERNATIONAL: pages 58, 61, 96, 98, 99, 114.

FRANK SPOONER PICTURES: pages 59, 64, 108 (bottom left and right), 109.

CAMERA PRESS: pages 63, 81 (left), 104, 108 (top left), 111, 121

THE BRIDGEMAN ART LIBRARY *'Ask Me No More' by Lawrence Alma-Tadema (1836–1912)*: page 66.

MARY EVANS PICTURE LIBRARY: pages 68, 124, 126, 127 (plus Horoscopes pages 92–95).

BBC HULTON PICTURE LIBRARY: page 70.

ALPHA: pages 72, 83, 117, 119.

THE PHOTO SOURCE: pages 71, 103 (bottom).

THE TATE GALLERY, LONDON *'The Kiss' by Rodin*: page 76.

PEOPLE IN PICTURES: pages 80 (right), 81 (right), 88, 91, 107, 108 (top right).

DEREK W RIDGERS: pages 80 (left), 82, 84, 85, 86, 118.

ASSOCIATED PRESS: pages 100, 103 (top).

PRESSEAGENTER: page 105.

DOISNEAU/RAPHO: page 113.